Y0-AGT-481

HAL

MENINGITIS

Other titles in Diseases and People

AIDS
0-7660-1182-8

ALLERGIES
0-7660-1048-1

ANOREXIA AND BULIMIA
0-7660-1047-3

ASTHMA
0-89490-712-3

CANCER
0-7660-1181-X

CARPAL TUNNEL SYNDROME AND OTHER REPETITIVE STRAIN INJURIES
0-7660-1184-4

CHICKENPOX AND SHINGLES
0-89490-715-8

COMMON COLD AND FLU
0-89490-463-9

DEPRESSION
0-89490-713-1

DIABETES
0-89490-464-7

EPILEPSY
0-7660-1049-X

FOOD POISONING AND FOODBORNE DISEASES
0-7660-1183-6

HEART DISEASE
0-7660-1051-1

HEPATITIS
0-89490-467-1

LYME DISEASE
0-7660-1052-X

MEASLES AND RUBELLA
0-89490-714-X

MONONUCLEOSIS
0-89490-466-3

MULTIPLE SCLEROSIS
0-7660-1185-2

RABIES
0-89490-465-5

SEXUALLY TRANSMITTED DISEASES
0-7660-1050-3

SICKLE CELL ANEMIA
0-89490-711-5

TUBERCULOSIS
0-89490-462-0

—Diseases and People—

MENINGITIS

Edward Willett

Enslow Publishers, Inc.
40 Industrial Road   PO Box 38
Box 398   Aldershot
Berkeley Heights, NJ 07922 Hants GU12 6BP
USA   UK
http://www.enslow.com

Library of Congress Cataloging-in-Publication Data

Willett, Edward, 1959–
    Meningitis / Edward Willett.
       p. cm. — (Diseases and people)
    Includes bibliographical references and index.
    Summary: Discusses the history, symptoms, diagnosis, and treatment of meningitis
and examines ongoing research and its effect on the future treatment of this disease.
    ISBN 0-7660-1187-9
    1. Meningitis—Juvenile literature. [1. Meningitis. 2. Diseases.] I. Title. II. Series.
RC376.W54   1999
616.8'2—DC21   99-12279
                                         CIP

Printed in the United States of America

10 9 8 7 6 5 4 3 2 1

To Our Readers:
All Internet addresses in this book were active and appropriate when we went to press. Any
comments or suggestions can be sent by e-mail to Comments@enslow.com or to the address
on the back cover.

Illustration Credits: © Armando Waak, Pan American Health Organization/World
Health Organization, p. 72; © Corel Corporation, p. 50; Edward Willett, pp. 30,
33, 57, 61, 77; Enslow Publishers, Inc., pp. 10, 25, 41; National Cancer Institute,
p. 82; National Library of Medicine, pp. 16, 20, 45; © Skjold Photographs, p. 69;
William Andrews Clark Memorial Library, University of California, Los Angeles,
p. 13.

Cover Illustration: © TSM/Lester Lefkowitz, 1998

Contents

MENINGITIS

What is it? An inflammation of the lining of the brain and spinal cord, caused by various bacteria and viruses.

Who gets it? All ages, all races, both sexes. It is most common in children, young adults, and the elderly.

How do you get it? Most of the viruses and bacteria that cause meningitis live in the nose and throat. They are passed along by close contact with someone who is infected. Sharing eating utensils, drinking containers, lipstick, or cigarettes are examples of close contact. Another is kissing.

What are the symptoms? Headache, fever, vomiting, a stiff neck, sensitivity to light in the eyes, confusion, fatigue, and drowsiness. Septicemia, a serious complication of meningitis, shows up as a red or purple skin rash.

How is it treated? Most cases of viral meningitis cannot be treated; the patients must recover on their own. Fortunately, most recover fully. Bacterial meningitis is treated with large doses of antibiotics. The antibiotics used depend on which strain of bacteria is causing the disease. Drugs such as corticosteroids are sometimes given to reduce swelling. Pain medication relieves the sometimes agonizing headaches.

How can it be prevented? Good hygiene, especially frequent hand washing, is the most basic defense against both viral and bacterial meningitis. During outbreaks, avoid close contact with those who may have been exposed. Preventative doses of the antibiotic rifampin are often given to people who may have been exposed to someone with bacterial meningitis. The antibiotic kills the bacteria before they can cause the disease or infect someone else. Vaccines, of varying effectiveness, exist for some strains of bacterial meningitis, but not all.

1

A Fast, Deadly Disease

On March 11, 1992, ten-year-old Roger Hodden woke up feeling "out of sorts." He had a headache and threw up a couple of times, but he did not have a fever. His mother decided he was too sick to go to school. Instead, she took him to a baby-sitter until she could come back and pick him up at 3:30 P.M.

At the baby-sitter's home, Roger seemed listless. By lunchtime he was drowsy and running a fever. Knowing his mother would be back in the middle of the afternoon, the baby-sitter did not call a doctor. Roger's mother called a doctor as soon as she saw him, though, because by 3:30 he was not only sleepy, but also confused.

The doctor noticed a rash on Roger's chest, and that, along with all the other symptoms, convinced him to send Roger to the hospital immediately. Within hours, Roger's kidneys and other organs began to fail. The next day, he died.[1]

The disease that killed him with such frightening speed was not some rare tropical virus soon to star in a terrifying television movie. It was bacterial meningitis, a contagious disease that infects hundreds of thousands of people around the world every year. Three fourths of those infected are children.[2]

Meningitis is a general term for an infection of the meninges—the membranes covering the brain and spinal cord. Both viruses and bacteria can cause it, as can (rarely) fungi and protozoa.

Bacterial meningitis affects an estimated 20,000 people in the United States each year.[3] Another 30,000 to 50,000 people suffer from the much less dangerous viral meningitis.[4] Very rarely, head injuries, or allergic reactions to certain drugs also cause meningitis.

Bacterial meningitis is usually caused by one of three types of bacteria: *Streptococcus pneumoniae* (which also causes pneumonia), *Haemophilus influenzae* type b, and *Neisseria meningitidis*. *Haemophilus influenzae* type b used to be the most common cause of bacterial meningitis in North America, but a vaccine introduced in the mid-1980s has helped eliminate it. As a result, *Neisseria meningitidis* is now the most common cause.[5] Viral meningitis, meanwhile, can also be caused by the same viruses that cause such common childhood diseases as mumps, measles, and chicken pox. Among several others, a number of viruses commonly found in the intestines can also cause meningitis.

Of all the causes of meningitis, the most dangerous is *Neisseria meningitidis*. This bacterium lives in the throat, nose, and sinuses of 10 to 25 percent of all people without causing any symptoms.[6] However, it can also cause meningococcal disease, which can result in meningitis or a widespread infection of the body called meningococcemia. (Meningococcemia is the complication that killed Roger.) About twenty-six hundred cases of meningococcal disease occur each year in the United States. One in ten of the victims die.[7]

The cost of all forms of meningitis to society is enormous. Besides the pain and suffering of the victims and the grief of families whose loved ones die, there is the cost of large-scale vaccination whenever outbreaks of meningitis occur.

Some people who survive meningitis suffer long-term problems. These can include learning disabilities, deafness, speech disorders, language disorders, seizures, partial paralysis, diabetes, and blindness.[8] These disorders can put a strain on their families and friends.

Meningitis is an even more serious problem for people in developing countries, especially sub-Saharan Africa ("sub-Saharan" means south of the Sahara Desert). There, in the meningitis belt, large outbreaks of meningitis have occurred every eight to twelve years—and, since the 1980s, even more frequently. In the first half of 1996, in the worst epidemic on record, 111,280 cases of meningitis and 12,840 deaths were reported to the African Regional Office of the World Health Organization. Young children were affected most often. About half of those not treated quickly died.[9]

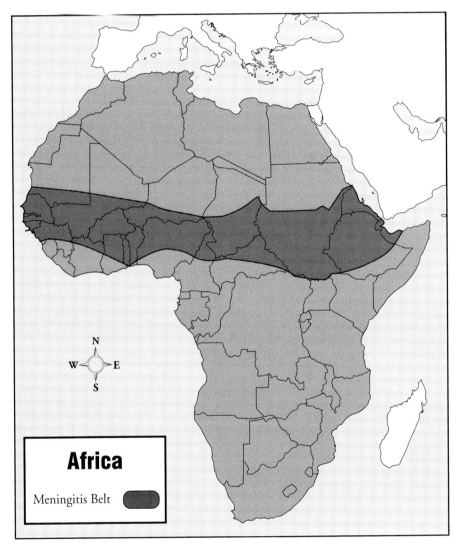

Meningitis is a serious problem for people south of the Sahara Desert in Africa, where outbreaks regularly occur in what is known as the meningitis belt.

Doctors and scientists are working hard to fight meningitis. Better hygiene, better education, and timely vaccination campaigns could greatly reduce the death rate in the meningitis belt, just as they have in North America. But wherever you are in the world, meningitis is always a potential threat. It is important to understand what meningitis is, what its symptoms are, how it can be treated, and how it can be prevented.

2

Meningitis Through the Ages

The Irish writer Oscar Wilde lived a century ago, but he is almost as famous today as he was then. His plays, such as *The Importance of Being Earnest* and *Lady Windermere's Fan*, are still performed. His most famous novel, *The Picture of Dorian Grey*, is still read and studied. He has been the subject of several recent books, a play, and even a movie.

He is also probably one of the most famous victims of meningitis: He died of the disease in Paris on November 30, 1900. He was only forty-six.[1]

In 1881, when Helen Keller was nineteen months old, she suffered from a disease that left her deaf and blind. Despite her handicaps, with the help of dedicated teacher Anne Sullivan, she learned to read, write, and speak. She lived until 1968, and gained international acclaim as a writer and lecturer. In 1991 *Life* magazine named her one of the one hundred most

In 1900, the Irish writer Oscar Wilde died from meningitis.

important Americans of the twentieth century. *The Miracle Worker*, a play based on her life, continues to be performed around the world. A movie version of *The Miracle Worker* won an Academy Award in 1962.

We cannot be sure, but many people believe that the disease that robbed Helen Keller of her eyesight and hearing was meningitis.[2]

Brain Fever

Meningitis has probably been around as long as there have been people, but nobody knew what caused it until the nineteenth century. Because they did not know what caused it, they did not call it meningitis, either. Instead, along with encephalitis (an inflammation of the brain) and typhus (a bacterial infection carried by lice and fleas that causes a high fever, headache, and skin rash), it was usually referred to as "brain fever."

Brain fever was common enough that many writers used it in their stories. Charles Dickens mentions it; so does Mark Twain. It shows up in one of the Sherlock Holmes's adventures written by Sir Arthur Conan Doyle, who was a doctor.

But as the nineteenth century progressed, doctors and scientists began to understand meningitis better. In 1806, Dr. Vieussuex, identified bacterial meningitis as a separate disease. However, he did not know what caused it, and he did not know how to treat it. At the time, bacterial meningitis killed almost everyone who contracted it.[3]

Meningitis was a very frightening disease at the time (even more frightening than it is now) because it was so often fatal, because there was no treatment, and because epidemics occurred every ten to twelve years. Though they did not know why, doctors noted that these epidemics hit young people hardest and happened more often during war. Because of this tendency, meningitis was called "a disease of children and soldiers."[4]

Developing a Treatment

Many different types of viruses and bacteria can cause meningitis. However, the bacteria called *Neisseria meningitidis,* also called meningococcal bacteria, cause the most dangerous form of meningitis. Meningococcal meningitis is particularly dangerous because sometimes the bacteria get into the bloodstream and cause a deadly infection, which can kill even a healthy young person in a day or two.

Austrian doctor Anton Weichselbaum identified *Neisseria meningitidis* as the cause of meningococcal meningitis in Germany in 1887.[5] He took samples of the spinal fluid of six patients suffering from meningitis and grew cultures of the bacteria he found. He then proved that those same bacteria caused meningitis in animals.[6] By identifying *Neisseria meningitidis* as the bacteria that caused the disease, he took the first step toward a treatment.

The first treatment for meningitis was serum therapy. Serum is the liquid part of the blood, in which the blood cells float. In the 1890s, scientists discovered that injecting the

15

Researchers test a meningitis serum on a mouse.

blood serum of a human or animal that had had a particular disease into another human or animal offered some protection against that disease. (The injected serum is called antiserum.) The protection occurs because when someone gets sick, the body creates substances called antibodies that are specifically designed to destroy the viruses or bacteria that are causing the sickness.

Dr. G. Jochmann, a German physician, made the first antiserum for *Neisseria meningitidis* in 1906.[7] Over the next few years, antiserums for meningitis became better and better as the various strains of bacteria that caused the disease were isolated. In fact, serum therapy was so successful that the death rate from meningitis caused by *Neisseria meningitidis* dropped from the usual 80 percent to just 30 percent.[8]

Epidemics Spur Research

During World War I (1914–1918), meningitis once again proved it deserved the name "a disease of children and soldiers." Widespread epidemics broke out in all the warring countries. The armed forces suffered most.[9] Epidemics were so common that the British Army tried to figure out how far apart soldiers' beds should be to minimize the risk of one soldier's infecting another by coughing or sneezing.[10]

These wartime epidemics resulted in a flurry of research. Scientists around the world raced to identify the various strains of *Neisseria meningitidis* causing the epidemics so they could make more effective antiserum.

They succeeded, but after the war research slowed. Meningitis antiserum continued to be produced, but the colonies of bacteria used to produce it were getting older and older. As the stock of bacteria aged, it no longer matched the bacteria causing the current disease. The antiserum produced from the old bacteria slowly became less effective.

Then, in 1928, a major epidemic broke out in China. The existing antiserum was useless against it. It spread across the world, moving to the Philippines, then right across the United States from west to east. A year later it swept into Great Britain and Europe.[11]

This epidemic proved that the world was still vulnerable to meningitis. Research resumed. Over the next few years scientists gained a better understanding of which strains of *Neisseria meningitidis* were involved in epidemics, and which were responsible for the few cases between epidemics. As a result, they were able to create much better antiserum.

And then something happened that made antiserum unnecessary.

Sulfa Drugs to the Rescue

Gerhard Domagk was a German biochemist, born in 1895. His research involved analyzing thousands of chemicals to see whether they could fight bacteria. In 1932 he tested a red dye called Prontosil.

The original dye did not seem to affect bacteria. However, when Domagk modified its chemical makeup slightly, it suddenly gained the ability to stop infections in mice caused by streptococcal bacteria.

Then Domagk's own daughter came down with an infection caused by that same type of bacteria. No drugs helped; she got sicker and sicker until it seemed likely she would die. Domagk dosed her with his modified version of Prontosil, and she made a complete recovery.[12]

After Domagk published his discovery in 1935, other doctors found that Prontosil contained a substance called sulfanilamide that could kill many other types of bacteria—including *Neisseria meningitidis*. Many new sulfa drugs that contained sulfanilamide were developed. The sulfa drugs revolutionized medicine and saved thousands of lives.[13] Not surprisingly, Domagk received the 1939 Nobel Prize in medicine for his discovery.

Even after penicillin became widely available a few years later, sulfa drugs continued for many years to be the antibiotics of choice for fighting meningitis. (Sometimes they were combined with penicillin.)[14] Today we have many more antibiotics to draw on.

At the beginning of World War II, F. S. Cheever discovered that giving antibiotics to people who had been exposed to *Neisseria meningitidis* before they got sick could wipe out any colonies of the bacteria they might be carrying. This kept them from infecting others, halting the development of an epidemic in its tracks. It was another important victory in the war against meningitis epidemics.

Vaccines: Better than Treatment

The introduction of antibiotics greatly reduced the death rate from bacterial meningitis.[15] Today, however, some strains of *Neisseria meningitidis* are becoming resistant to antibiotics. In 1974–75, for example, a massive meningitis epidemic struck Brazil, infecting more than 250,000 people and killing 11,000. One of the strains involved was resistant to antibiotics, which made fighting the epidemic very difficult.[16] Fortunately, the government of Brazil had another weapon in its arsenal: It vaccinated 80 million people against the disease.[17]

A vaccine is both similar to and different from an antiserum. A vaccine is made from weakened or killed bacteria, or

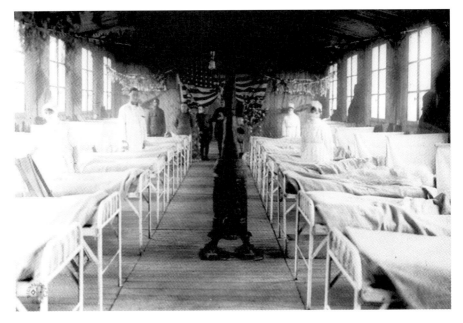

This United States Army Camp hospital had a meningitis ward to separate those with the contagious disease. Notice that the nurses are masked to help stop transmission of the disease.

sometimes (as in the case of meningococcal vaccines) just from specific molecules from the germ's outer wall.[18] When the vaccine is injected, the person's body thinks it is being infected, though it really is not. To fight off the fake infection, the body produces antibodies. Then if the live, active bacteria of the type used to make the vaccine appear, the person's body already contains antibodies against them. The antibodies destroy the bacteria before they can spread through the body and make the person sick.

During the meningitis epidemic of the late 1920s and early 1930s, scientists discovered that most of the meningitis caused by *Neisseria meningitidis* is the result of three main strains of bacteria, labeled a, b, and c. There are vaccines for types a and c, but none for type b.[19] Unfortunately, type b now causes more than half of all cases of *Neisseria meningitidis* infection in the United States and Europe.[20] However, most cases in deadly epidemics like the one in Brazil in the 1970s appear to be caused by type a, for which the vaccine works fairly well.

A Medical Milestone

Not all meningitis is caused by *Neisseria meningitidis.* Until recently, the most common cause of meningitis in small children was a bacterium called *Haemophilus influenzae* type b (Hib for short). Vaccination against Hib, however, has been so successful that life-threatening childhood Hib meningitis has practically disappeared.

As recently as a decade ago, up to twenty-five thousand children a year, most of them under five years old, used to contract Hib meningitis. More than a thousand children died of the disease every year. Many of those who survived suffered lifelong health problems, ranging from hearing loss to mental retardation.[21]

Today, Hib meningitis and other illnesses caused by the Hib bacteria have been virtually eliminated in countries that are able to vaccinate all children against the disease. In the first nine months of 1997, only 175 cases of Hib meningitis were reported in the entire United States.[22]

One of the most amazing things about the Hib vaccine is that researchers had been trying to create it for half a century. In 1930, scientists discovered a new way to make a vaccine. They linked molecules called polysaccharides, found on the outer wall of bacteria, with a particular protein. When they injected this into mice, the mice produced antibodies against the bacteria the polysaccharides came from.[23]

About the same time, researchers began to search for a vaccine that would protect children and infants against Hib bacteria. For decades, that search proved fruitless. But in the late 1960s, scientists figured out the details of the bacteria's polysaccharide coat. They began to develop vaccines based on that discovery.[24]

The first Hib vaccines appeared in the 1970s. Unfortunately, they only worked in adults. Further research finally yielded a vaccine that was 85 to 90 percent effective in children eighteen months and older. But the vaccine still did not work in infants.

In 1985, doctors started vaccinating children two years old and older with the vaccine. In 1987 new versions of the vaccine that worked in children as young as two months old were licensed. Today, almost all children in the United States are routinely vaccinated at two, four, and six months of age, with a booster at fifteen months.[25]

There is also a vaccine for the third most common cause of bacterial meningitis, *Streptococcus pneumoniae*. Unfortunately, it is not as effective as the Hib vaccine, and it does not work well for children younger than two years. Usually it is given only to people older than sixty-five (who are particularly vulnerable to this form of meningitis) or to those with other serious health problems that make them vulnerable.[26] However, several new vaccines are in development. Doctors hope they will prove as successful as the Hib vaccine.

For meningitis caused by viruses, nothing has changed over the years. There are no vaccines. The only treatment is to make the patient as comfortable as possible. Fortunately, most victims of viral meningitis recover completely.

A Remarkable Success

Bacterial meningitis remains a dangerous, sometimes deadly disease. In many parts of the developing world, it continues to sicken and kill hundreds of thousands of people a year.

In North America, however, though meningitis still kills many people annually, it is far less of a threat than it once was. The epidemics that used to sweep across the country every decade or so seem to have been eliminated.

According to Dr. Bradley Perkins, a meningitis specialist at the federal Centers for Disease Control and Prevention (CDC), the United States' efforts to fight meningitis with knowledge, antibiotics, and vaccines are "a remarkable public-health success."[27]

3

What Is Meningitis?

Nicola, a twenty-three-year-old secretary, went to her doctor one morning because she had a bad headache and was throwing up. The doctor examined her and found she had a slight fever and that the light hurt her eyes. However, he did not become alarmed until he asked her to bend her chin down to her chest. She could not; her neck was too stiff.

The doctor immediately diagnosed her as having meningitis and gave her a shot of penicillin. Then he called an ambulance to rush her to the hospital. Tests confirmed she had viral meningitis. She was given painkillers to relieve the agonizing headaches. She stayed in the hospital until the infection was gone.

She was very tired and listless for many days, but about a month after she became ill she was able to return to work, completely recovered.[1]

A Not-So-Silver Lining

Meningitis is a swelling of the meninges, the lining surrounding the brain and spinal cord. Any one of several different viruses or bacteria can cause it. More rarely, so can some fungi and protozoa. Sometimes meningitis is even caused by a blow to the head; blood enters the meninges and causes them to swell.

What Are the Meninges?

The meninges are protective wrappings around the brain and spinal cord. There are three layers that run from the forebrain (the front part of the brain) to the spinal cord. Some people call meningitis "spinal meningitis," but there really is no such thing. Meningitis always involves the covering of the brain as well.[2]

The innermost layer of the meninges is called the pia mater. It looks like a very fine mesh. It is made up

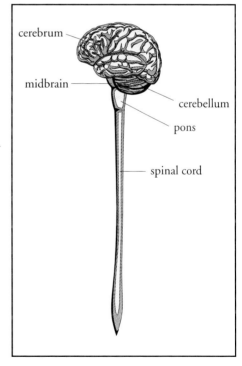

Meningitis occurs when the lining around the brain and the spinal cord—the meninges—becomes swollen.

25

mostly of tiny blood vessels, which cling to the surface of the brain and spinal cord as tightly as plastic wrap clings to food. The outermost layer is tough and shiny, and is called the dura mater.

Between those two layers is the arachnoid layer, which covers the brain very loosely. Unlike the pia mater, it does not slip down into the dips and folds that cover the brain's surface. The arachnoid layer is filled with between 100 and 160 milliliters (less in children) of cerebrospinal fluid (CSF). CSF is a liquid that helps cushion the brain against jolts and blows to the head.[3]

It is very rare for the dura mater to be infected. When it does happen (usually as a side effect of a skull fracture), the infection usually stays in a small area and does not affect the other meninges or the brain itself.[4]

In most cases of meningitis, the infection takes hold in the CSF. Because the CSF has very few white blood cells or antibodies in it, viruses and bacteria there are able to multiply rapidly.[5]

The Most Common Form

Viral meningitis (sometimes called aseptic meningitis) is the most common form of meningitis. Exactly how many cases of viral meningitis occur in the United States each year is hard to say. Many mild cases may have symptoms very similar to that of influenza, so they may never be reported to a doctor. Between 1987 and 1994, according to figures from the CDC,

11,172 cases of severe viral meningitis were reported annually.[6] From that, the CDC estimates there are between 30,000 and 50,000 cases of viral meningitis a year in the United States.[7]

More than half the viral meningitis cases in the United States are caused by the Coxsackie virus and echovirus. Both are normally found in the intestines. The herpes simplex, measles, polio, and chicken pox viruses can also cause meningitis.

Recovery from viral meningitis is usually as complete as it was in Nicola's case.

Bacterial Meningitis

As a rule, meningitis caused by bacteria is much more serious than meningitis caused by viruses. Although we now have antibiotics to fight bacterial meningitis, it still kills hundreds of people every year in the United States and many thousands worldwide.

Just as more than one type of virus causes viral meningitis, more than one type of bacteria causes bacterial meningitis. In fact, nearly fifty species of bacteria have been reported to occasionally cause meningitis.[8] However, the majority of cases are caused by one of three types: *Neisseria meningitidis* (meningococcal), *Streptococcus pneumoniae* (pneumococcal), and *Haemophilus influenzae* type b (Hib).

For the past ten years, cases of pneumococcal meningitis have remained steady at 1.1 cases per 100,000 people. Hib meningitis has dropped from 2.9 cases per 100,000 in 1986 to

The Difference Between Bacteria and Viruses

Bacteria are tiny living creatures so small they can only be seen through a microscope. They can do many of the things larger creatures do, including eat and reproduce. They reproduce by splitting in two, and they can reproduce very rapidly. Bacteria are around us all the time. Most are harmless and many are even helpful. However, some of them, when they get inside our bodies, start to eat our tissues or produce poisons that can make us very sick. When harmful bacteria attack our bodies, we have an infection.

Viruses are much, much smaller than bacteria, and they do not reproduce the same way. Each bacterium has a set of organelles that work just like our own organs. Viruses do not have any organelles. To reproduce, they have to burrow into another living cell and take over its organelles, using them to make more viruses. This process kills the cell, which then bursts open, releasing hundreds of more viruses. The death of cells and the side effects of our bodies' efforts to fight viruses make us sick. Viruses cause many other diseases besides meningitis, including measles, chicken pox, mumps, AIDS, influenza, and the common cold.[9]

just 0.2 cases per 100,000 in 1995, thanks to a very effective vaccine introduced in the 1980s.[10]

However, meningococcal meningitis, the most dangerous form, is becoming more common. In 1996, there were 3,437 cases reported in the United States, a 47 percent increase from ten years earlier.[11]

All three of the bacteria that most commonly cause meningitis live harmlessly in the noses and throats of many people. In some people, however, for reasons not well understood, they manage to get into the central nervous system and infect the meninges. The body's attempt to rid itself of this infection produces the symptoms of meningitis.

Fighting for Its Life

When it is fighting an infection, the body has several strategies. White blood cells, for example, attempt to "eat" infectious bacteria, swallowing them and destroying them. The body also releases antibodies. Whereas white blood cells attack anything foreign, antibodies are designed to attack specific bacteria or viruses.

White blood cells communicate with each other by releasing chemicals called cytokines. There are many different kinds of cytokines. One of them, called histamine, makes blood vessels dilate, allowing more blood and fluid to enter an infected area. This helps white blood cells reach the infection, but also causes redness and swelling. In meningitis, the swelling of the brain's lining puts pressure on the brain, causing headaches.

Meningitis often crops up in boarding schools, where many students are in close proximity day after day. The bacteria that cause meningitis can live in the noses and throats of many people.

A different cytokine causes the body's temperature to rise. The goal is to make things too hot for the infecting bacteria or viruses to survive. We call this rising temperature a fever.

Finally, another cytokine makes white blood cells release enzymes that dissolve the bacteria in the blood. Unfortunately, these enzymes can also damage surrounding tissue. When the meninges are infected, the surrounding tissue includes nerve cells. Damage to nerve cells can cause facial paralysis, loss of vision and hearing, mental confusion, and drowsiness.

A Deadly Side Effect

Normally, the body turns off the cytokines as the infection is cleared, and then gets rid of them in the urine. However, if the infection is severe enough, so many cytokines may be released that the body cannot get rid of them fast enough to avoid widespread tissue damage. This condition, called septic shock, kills many of the people who die of a *Neisseria meningitidis* infection. When *Neisseria meningitidis* infects the bloodstream, the person is said to have meningococcemia.

Since all three of the bacteria that commonly cause meningitis live mainly in the nose and throat, they can be passed from one person to another, much like a cold virus, in fluid from the nose and mouth. Two people can pass the germs back and forth by sharing a knife, fork, spoon, or drinking glass, or by kissing, sneezing, or coughing.[12] For that reason, whenever there is an outbreak of meningitis, people are urged to avoid sharing anything that contacts the mouth, eyes, or nose.

31

For example, when six cases of bacterial meningitis surfaced in Ontario in December 1997, the Waterloo Minor Peewee Mighty Ducks hockey team issued individual plastic squirt-bottles for each player. Before that, bottles were shared.[13]

Good hygiene, especially washing hands frequently, is probably the most important thing anyone can do to avoid getting meningitis (or, for that matter, a cold).

Some Are Lucky, Others Are Not

No one is sure why some people get meningitis and others do not, even though they have been exposed to the same germs. Normally, the body keeps germs out of the meninges with the blood-brain barrier. This barrier is a result of the fact that the tiny blood vessels that feed the brain will only let certain substances through. Even white blood cells and antibodies have a hard time getting through the blood-brain barrier, and as a rule, germs do not make it through at all. Once they do, however, and start growing in the CSF, it is very hard for the body to fight them.[14]

One theory about why some people get meningitis and others do not is that people who have recently been sick are more vulnerable because their immune systems are already weakened. Bacterial meningitis is more common in the winter, notes Dr. Ann Schuchat, acting chief of the CDC's respiratory-diseases branch. Winter is when many other germs—especially those that cause colds and influenza (flu)—are more prevalent. "It

During meningitis outbreaks, school students are warned about the dangers of sharing eating utensils and drink containers.

may be that winter viruses reduce our defenses against the bacteria," she said.[15]

Another theory is that in some people, the brain is not as well sealed off as it should be. In everyone's head, there are many places where nerves, arteries, and veins enter the skull. Maybe tiny defects in the seals surrounding these nerves, arteries, and veins where they enter the skull allow germs to sneak in.

One place this could happen is where the nerves responsible for our sense of smell pass into the base of the brain from the nose. There is a plate of bone there called the cribriform plate. In some people, germs may be able to get through the cribriform plate from the nose. This route of infection would explain why the bacteria that most commonly cause meningitis usually live harmlessly in the nose and throat.[16]

Other organisms besides the viruses and bacteria mentioned so far can cause meningitis. Some of these rarer types of meningitis, a few of which are listed on the following pages, are among the most deadly.

Neonatal Meningitis

Neonatal means "newborn." Neonatal meningitis is meningitis occurring in newborn infants. Two bacteria are most often responsible for this type of meningitis, Group B Streptococcus (GBS) and *Escherichia coli* (*E. coli*).

GBS is the most common cause of life-threatening infections in newborns. In addition to meningitis, it can cause blood infection and pneumonia. Approximately 8,000 babies in the United States get one of these forms of GBS disease every year. Between 400 and 1,200 die.

Many people carry GBS in their bodies without becoming ill. Instead, they are colonized. In a colonized adult, the bacteria may live in the large intestine, the genital tract, the urinary tract, the throat, or the respiratory tract. Between 15 and 40 percent of pregnant women are colonized with GBS in the rectum or vagina. During birth, the baby's skin may pick up some of these bacteria. Approximately one to 2 percent of babies who are colonized this way develop GBS disease.

GBS disease causes meningitis most often in babies who develop it one week to several months after birth. Only half of these babies pick up the GBS bacteria from their mothers. No one knows where the other babies pick up GBS.

GBS disease in all its forms can be treated with antibiotics. Pregnant women colonized with the GBS bacteria are often treated with antibiotics before the baby is born, to kill off the bacteria before they can be passed on to the baby.

E. coli, the other bacteria that most often cause meningitis in newborn babies, are commonly found in the intestines. Sometimes they cause urinary tract infections and diarrhea. Eating food contaminated with *E. coli* can result in food poisoning. For example, *E. coli* contamination in ground meat has caused a form of food poisoning that has killed several people over the past few years. *E. coli* meningitis is also treated with antibiotics.

Staphylococcal Meningitis

Staphylococcal meningitis is a very serious form of meningitis caused by *Staphylococcus aureus*. It usually develops as a complication of surgery. People who have had previous brain infections have the greatest risk of developing staphylococcal meningitis and are sometimes given antibiotics before surgery to reduce that risk.

Tuberculosis (TB) Meningitis

The same bacteria that cause tuberculosis cause TB meningitis. Usually the infection starts somewhere else (typically the lungs), then spreads to the meninges. People at particular risk for TB meningitis include the elderly, young children, people with HIV/AIDS, and anyone from a region where tuberculosis is common.

Cryptococcal Meningitis

Cryptococcal meningitis is a rare but very serious form of meningitis that is caused by a fungus. *Cryptococcus neoformans* is a type of yeast found in soil around the world. Only five out of every one million people develop cryptococcal meningitis. They are almost always people whose immune systems are not working very well. That could be because of a disease, such as AIDS or leukemia, or because of some medical treatment, such as chemotherapy to treat cancer or the drugs given after organ transplants to prevent rejection.

Cryptococcal meningitis can be treated with drugs that kill fungi.

Syphilitic Meningitis

Syphilitic meningitis is even rarer than cryptococcal meningitis: Only two out of every one million people suffer from it. It occurs in people who have already contracted syphilis, a disease that is usually transmitted through sexual contact.

Syphilitic meningitis is a very severe form of meningitis that can lead to permanent brain damage and life-threatening seizures. It is treated with antibiotics.

Other Causes

Karen, twenty-two, suffered from meningitis more than once. Within eight months, she was in the hospital three times, deathly ill. Each time she was given antibiotic treatment, and she recovered completely. However, the disease kept coming back.[17]

Her doctors ruled out all the causes of meningitis already presented in this chapter. Then they looked at even rarer causes. *Naegleria fowleri*, for instance, is a rare amoeba (a type of microscopic animal) that sometimes lives in stagnant fresh-water ponds. It can infect people who bathe or swim in the pond—but that did not apply to Karen. Brain, skull, and spinal injuries sometimes lead to recurring meningitis if a pocket of infection lingers near where the injury occurred—but Karen had not hurt her head. Nor did she have Lyme disease, an illness spread by ticks that sometimes causes meningitis.[18]

Eventually her doctors figured it out. Karen had one of the rarest forms of meningitis of all. She was allergic to ibuprofen, the active ingredient in many pain-relieving medicines, including Motrin®, Advil®, Nuprin®, and Medipren®. The antibiotics had not done anything to cure her: Time had done that by itself.[19]

As you can see, meningitis is a disease that can be caused by many different things. Its many possible causes can make it very hard to diagnose and treat.

Diagnosis of Meningitis

Sarah, a ninth-grade student, woke up one Monday morning feeling as if she were coming down with a cold. She went to school anyway.

By midmorning she had developed a mild headache, and her cold seemed worse, so she went to the school nurse. The nurse did not think there was anything seriously wrong and sent her back to class. By late afternoon, though, Sarah felt terrible. Her back and neck felt stiff. As the afternoon progressed, she became mentally confused and started vomiting. The alarmed school nurse rushed Sarah to the hospital emergency room. A test called a spinal tap confirmed the nurse's worst suspicion: Sarah had bacterial meningitis. Fortunately, after being hospitalized and treated with antibiotics, she recovered completely.[1]

At First It Looks Like the Flu

The early symptoms of meningitis are often very similar to those caused by "winter viruses" like the flu and colds. The similarity adds greatly to the danger posed by the disease. Too often, people ignore the symptoms, thinking they have an ordinary respiratory infection. Unfortunately, with bacterial meningitis, every minute without treatment increases the danger.[2]

The symptoms of meningitis are different in adults and children, and not everyone exhibits the same symptoms. This makes meningitis even more difficult to diagnose. In adults and teenagers, doctors look for the classic triad: fever, neck stiffness, and impaired consciousness (confusion and drowsiness). The real giveaway is the neck stiffness. It is not just a generalized stiffness of the neck like you might get from sleeping the wrong way on your pillow. With meningitis, bending your head forward onto your chest becomes difficult and painful.

However, a recent study of adult cases of meningitis discovered that only 51 percent of patients had all three symptoms. The majority had a fever above 100.4 degrees Fahrenheit, 82 percent had neck stiffness, and two thirds showed signs of impaired consciousness.[3]

In infants, doctors look for symptoms such as fever, irritability, and seizures, because the classic triad usually is not present. Babies have a soft spot on the front of their head called the fontanel. Sometimes in an infant with meningitis the fontanel will be forced slightly outward because of the swelling of the brain underneath. However, that occurs in less

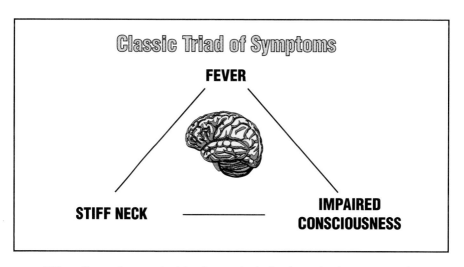

When diagnosing meningitis, doctors look for three classic symptoms in teens and adults: fever, stiff neck, and impaired consciousness.

than 50 percent of newborns. (The fontanel also bulges out when a baby is crying. For that reason, it is important to check the fontanel when the baby is quiet.[4]) Even fever, which shows up in almost all adults with meningitis, occurs in less than half of newborns with the disease. The older the child, the more likely the classic triad will be present.[5]

Besides causing meningitis, *Neisseria meningitidis* can cause meningococcemia, a dangerous blood infection that can kill within hours. The primary symptom of meningococcemia, in both adults and children, is a rash with spots that do not turn white when pressed.

Not all these symptoms necessarily occur at the same time, and not everyone develops all of the symptoms. The most important thing to remember is that if you think

Symptoms of Meningitis[6]

IN ADULTS
- Fever
- Vomiting
- Headache
- Drowsiness and confusion
- Seizures
- Stiff neck and joint pain
- Eyes sensitive to light

IN CHILDREN
- A high-pitched moaning cry or whimpering
- Dislike of being handled, fretful behavior
- Arching back
- Blank, staring expression
- Difficult to wake up or very lethargic
- Fever, and cold hands and feet
- Refusing food or vomiting
- Pale, blotchy skin color

you or someone you know might have meningitis or meningococcemia, see a doctor immediately.

Only One Way to Be Sure

Although doctors might suspect meningitis, the only way to be certain that a particular patient is suffering from that disease is to perform a test called a spinal tap, also known as a lumbar puncture.

The surface of the brain and spine are bathed in a liquid called the cerebrospinal fluid (CSF). This fluid cushions the brain and spinal cord from damaging jolts. The CSF is warm and rich in sugars and proteins, good sources of food for bacteria. If bacteria get into the CSF, they grow well.[7]

A spinal tap allows doctors to examine the CSF to see whether it contains meningitis-causing bacteria, viruses, or fungi and, if so, which organism is present.[8]

Doctors learn many other things from spinal taps, as well. Fluid pressure is important: Above-normal pressure in the CSF indicates that there may be a massive infection in the meninges or in the brain itself.[9]

The CSF is also analyzed for blood cells, protein, and glucose. In any form of meningitis, the number of white blood cells and the protein level are usually higher than normal. In the case of bacterial meningitis, the glucose level is usually lower than normal. To discover the specific organism causing the meningitis, the CSF is examined under a microscope and cultured.[10] Some of it is placed in a dish containing a mixture of nutrients. As the organism multiplies in the nutrient mixture, it can be more easily identified.

Even before these tests are carried out, though, a doctor can usually tell whether the patient has bacterial meningitis just by looking at the CSF. It is normally clear, but in people suffering from bacterial meningitis, it is usually cloudy, because it contains bacteria and white blood cells.[11]

The Spinal Tap

During a spinal tap, a doctor inserts a small, hollow needle through the space between the patient's two vertebrae (the bones of the spine). A small sample of cerebrospinal fluid is allowed to drip into a series of sample tubes.[12] The procedure is also called a lumbar puncture because the needle is inserted in the lower, or lumbar, part of the spine, below the place where the spinal cord ends. That way there is no risk of damaging the cord.[13]

During a spinal tap the patient lies curled up on his or her side, with knees and thighs bent. This opens the spaces between the lumbar vertebrae. Young children sometimes have to be held in this position, because they tend to be very sick and irritable by the time a spinal tap is done. Small infants are sometimes placed in a sitting position with the head slightly flexed or supported with a pillow propped between the arms and legs.[14]

The skin over the chosen spot is carefully cleaned with an antibacterial solution. Sometimes it is also numbed slightly with a topical anesthetic.

"Extreme care and cleanliness are always used when doing a lumbar puncture," said Dr. Frederick Meier, chairman of the pathology department of the Alfred I. duPont Hospital for Children in Wilmington, Delaware. "And the procedure is done as rapidly as possible to minimize discomfort."[15]

Once the test is over, a small bandage is applied to the tiny puncture wound. After that, patients usually receive additional fluids and are asked to lie flat and limit their activities for a few

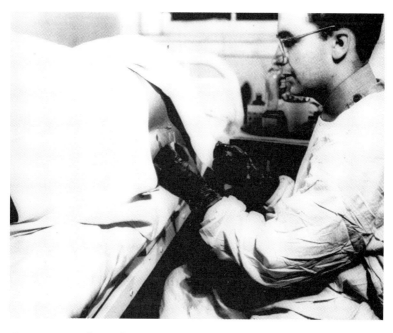

During a spinal tap, the patient lies on his side while the doctor inserts a needle into the space between the bones of the spine. Cerebrospinal fluid is collected for analysis.

days. This is to limit any more leaking of CSF from the puncture wound. (If CSF pressure drops too low, a patient can get a very bad headache.)

Some results, such as cell counts, are ready within minutes or hours; cultures may take two to three days, depending on how slow-growing the organism is.[16] Fortunately, bacterial meningitis can often be confirmed quickly.

Sometimes an additional test, a computerized tomographic (CT) scan, is necessary. A cat scan (as it is pronounced) reveals the inner structure of the brain and can show whether there are other problems, such as a tumor, that could account for the meningitis-like symptoms.

The Deadly Rash

Matt Faria, seventeen, of Framingham, Massachusetts, spent one January evening moving furniture, and then doing homework. He felt fine then, but at 2 A.M. he woke his mother: He had developed a fever of 103 degrees Fahrenheit. She gave him Advil®, and his fever dropped, but soon it was up again.

At noon the next day, his parents took Matt to the hospital. By that time, Matt could hardly stand up. Half an hour later he broke out in a red rash, which quickly became purplish, blotchy bruising all over his body.

Dr. Thomas Treadwell, chief of infectious disease at Metro West Hospital in Framingham, took one look and knew Matt was very ill. "Everybody, let's get masks on and let's get going," he said. The emergency room team took Matt away. Then someone took Matt's parents out into the hall and told them their son might very well die.[17]

Meningitis itself does not produce any outward changes to the body, but when meningitis is caused by bacteria that finds its way into the bloodstream, a telltale rash can develop. (This occurs most often when the bacteria involved is *Neisseria meningitidis*, but it can occur with both pneumococcal and Hib meningitis as well.[18]) As Dr. Treadwell knew, the rash is a very bad sign.

The rash is a symptom that the body's immune system is out of control. Whenever the body is fighting an infection, the walls of the blood vessels become more porous. This lets white blood cells and antibodies more easily enter infected tissue. But in very serious, overwhelming infections, like meningococcemia, the blood vessels become so porous that blood pours into the skin and internal organs. This shows up on the surface of the skin as a purplish rash that does not change color when pressed. The combination of leaky blood vessels, poisons produced by the bacteria, and the cytokines released by white blood cells can cause blood pressure to be dangerously low.

The rash initially looks like clusters of tiny pin pricks, but as the disease progresses, it may develop into huge purple blotches, a sign that the patient is in serious trouble.[19]

Matt Faria was in very serious trouble. For two weeks, he was in a coma, being pumped full of antibiotics and other drugs. All that time he was hooked up to a dialysis machine, which helped clean the poisons from his bloodstream. His skin blackened and died in some of the areas where the purplish blotches appeared. As a result, he had to have many skin grafts and other surgeries. His legs suffered permanent damage. Nevertheless, he survived.[20] Fortunately for Matt, both bacterial meningitis and the deadly systemwide infection that sometimes develops along with it can be treated.

5

Treatment of Meningitis

Virginia, a twenty-two-year-old college student, had been fighting the flu for a couple of days when, one morning at 4 A.M., she woke up with a terrible headache. She threw up. By 7 A.M. she was delirious. Her parents called an ambulance.

Because of the headache, the doctor in the emergency room immediately suspected meningitis and ordered a massive dose of antibiotics. When he discovered a rash on Virginia's chest, he knew he was dealing not just with meningitis but with meningococcemia, which can kill within hours. A spinal tap confirmed his diagnosis. By then she was in a comatose state.

For the next twenty-four hours, the hospital staff kept a close watch on Virginia's condition. If her blood pressure dropped or the rash grew worse, it would mean poisons from the bacteria that had caused her meningitis were spreading throughout her system. Fortunately, her blood pressure held steady.

Three days later, Virginia opened her eyes. Prompt treatment had saved her life.[1]

Shoot First and Ask Questions Later

Whenever doctors suspect meningitis, they administer antibiotics. Bacterial meningitis is so dangerous that it demands "a shoot-first-ask-questions-later approach," said Dr. Tony Dajer, who treated Virginia in the emergency room.[2]

If a virus is causing the meningitis, however, antibiotics do no good. Although antiviral drugs are helpful against certain viruses that can cause meningitis (a drug called acyclovir can fight meningitis caused by the herpes simplex virus, for instance),[3] for most cases of viral meningitis, there is no treatment. Instead, over time, the body simply has to fight off the invading viruses on its own.[4]

All a doctor can do for most cases of viral meningitis is make patients as comfortable as possible. Almost all patients receive pain-relieving drugs to help them deal with the agonizing headache that accompanies the disease.

Antibiotics Give Hope

Fortunately, most people who suffer from viral meningitis recover completely. People suffering from bacterial meningitis, however, usually die without treatment, so it is even more

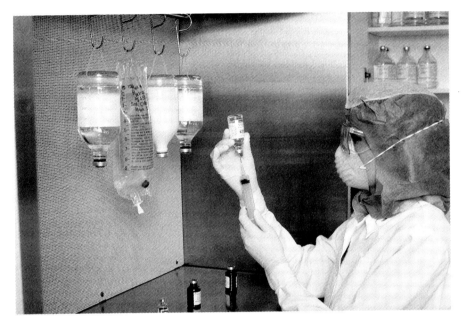

Intravenous antibiotics are given to patients to treat bacterial meningitis.

fortunate that antibiotics can be used to successfully treat the disease in most cases.

Since some strains of the various bacteria that cause meningitis have developed resistance to certain antibiotics over the years (see "Super Bacteria on the Rise" on page 52), a mixture of several different antibiotics is often administered.[5] However, once the specific type of bacteria causing the disease has been determined, treatment may be narrowed to one or two antibiotics known to be particularly effective against that bacterium.[6]

Ceftriaxone and cefotaxime are usually used first. Other drugs that may be used include ampicillin and vancomycin.

The antibiotics are usually delivered intravenously (which means they are dripped directly into the bloodstream through a needle inserted into a vein in the patient's arm).

It takes a lot of antibiotics to fight off bacterial meningitis. The blood-brain barrier keeps most of the antibiotics out of the CSF, so large doses are required to get enough through the barrier to do any good. By way of comparison, a single dose of 1.2 million units of penicillin is usually enough to cure a strep throat. A patient suffering from meningitis requires twenty times that much every day to successfully fight off the infection.[7]

No Guarantees

Even with antibiotics, there are no guarantees that the treatment of any specific case of meningitis will be successful.

One reason antibiotics do not always work is that some types of bacteria release toxins that continue to damage the body even after the bacteria themselves are dead.[8] The earlier in the course of the disease the patient receives antibiotics, the better the results.[9]

In addition to antibiotics, people suffering from meningitis are often given intravenous corticosteroids.[10] These drugs reduce swelling in the brain, which can reduce pain and the risk of brain damage. They may also reduce the damage caused by bacterial toxins and cytokines.

Patients with meningitis (or any other serious illness) are closely watched all the time using the "ABC" approach: airway, breathing, and circulation. In other words, the goal is always to make sure their hearts and lungs are working normally.

Super Bacteria on the Rise

Today when patients arrive in the emergency room with the symptoms of meningitis, they are given ceftriaxone and cefotaxime first. A few years ago, the first choice would have been penicillin. It is not now because *Streptococcus pneumoniae*, one type of meningitis-causing bacteria, is increasingly resistant to penicillin.

Bacteria of all sorts are becoming resistant to antibiotics. No antibiotic kills every single bacterium. The bacteria that survive have a natural immunity to that antibiotic's effects. When they reproduce, they pass on that immunity.

Heavy use of antibiotics in the past has resulted in more and more antibiotics losing their effectiveness against certain germs. For example, up to 45 percent of *Streptococcus pneumoniae* bacteria are resistant to penicillin. About 30 percent of Hib bacteria are resistant to ampicillin.

Even ceftriaxone and cefotaxime, today's meningitis-fighting antibiotics of choice, offer no guarantees: Up to 15 percent of *Streptococcus pneumoniae* may be resistant to them, too.

One reason antibiotic resistance has developed is that some people misuse antibiotics. Many people take them every time they have a cold or the flu—even though those diseases, which are caused by viruses, are not helped by antibiotics. Sometimes people do not take all the pills in their antibiotic prescriptions once their symptoms disappear. The more resistant germs may then survive and pass their resistance to their offspring.

Germs may be emerging now that are resistant to all the antibiotics currently known. If that happens, diseases like meningitis and even minor infections people sometimes get from a simple cut may prove deadly more and more often.

Complications doctors watch for include dehydration, low blood pressure, seizures, and hydrocephalus (swelling of the brain due to a buildup of fluid).[11]

There is no fixed rule, but antibiotic treatment generally continues for at least ten to fourteen days. A period of three to four days without fever and with very few other symptoms, such as headache or vomiting, indicates the infection is gone.[12]

Four weeks after she opened her eyes, Virginia was back at work but she still suffered from headaches. "They make her think the meningitis is coming back. They scare her," her mother said.[13]

Fortunately, it is very unusual for meningitis to occur in the same person twice. But considering how frightening meningitis can be, even with modern treatment, it is no wonder those who survive worry they might be stricken again.

6

Meningitis and Society

The biggest impact of meningitis on society can be summed up in one word: fear. Whenever people think there has been an outbreak of the disease, they tend to panic. A perfect example of this is what happened in Rhode Island in early 1998.

In 1996, there was an outbreak of meningococcal disease, both meningitis and meningococcemia, in Woonsocket, Rhode Island. Within four weeks, there were four cases. One sixteen-year-old boy died. In response, the state vaccinated seventeen thousand schoolchildren against *Neisseria meningitidis*. During that year, Rhode Island recorded twenty-three cases of meningococcal disease and two deaths from it.[1] That total was noticeably higher than in the previous three years. In 1997, the total remained high: There were twenty-four cases of meningococcal disease, and nine people died.[2]

None of the Rhode Island cases got much publicity, so the public was not very concerned. Health officials, however, were watching the situation closely. Then, on January 12, 1998, a two-and-a-half-year-old girl, Jessica Lee McMahon, of East Providence, died of what was probably meningococcal disease ("probably," because laboratory tests could not confirm it).[3] Exactly one month later, nine-year-old Jorge Candelario of Woonsocket—where the outbreak had occurred a year and a half earlier—also died. Although the two cases were not related, and there was no evidence that a new outbreak was occurring, state health officials decided to vaccinate all the schoolchildren in the city who had not been vaccinated in 1996.[4]

The officials made an announcement at a televised news conference. They told people there was no outbreak, because the two cases were unrelated and the number of cases was no higher than usual. They made it clear that Jorge's death was not connected to the 1996 outbreak. They also explained that the strain of the bacteria that caused his death had never been known to cause an outbreak. However, people did not listen to their reassurances. Convinced that their children were in danger of contracting meningitis, parents across the state remained fearful.[5]

Reacting to public concern, politicians demanded that the CDC send a team to Rhode Island. The CDC eventually agreed, although it already knew about the situation and was not concerned. The politicians also crafted a bill that required all children to be vaccinated against meningococcal disease before entering school.[6]

To alleviate concerns, the state health department sent out a press release encouraging people to vaccinate their children. They even urged insurance companies to pay for it. But instead of reassuring people, their announcement only made them more worried, because just a couple of hours after the press release went out, a five-year-old boy from North Providence died of a meningococcal infection. That made it look as if the press release had been sent out in response to his death, even though it had not. In fact, tests later showed that he had died of a different strain of the disease than Jorge had.[7]

Worry became panic. Parents started lining up at medical clinics, demanding vaccinations for their children. Clinics that had the vaccine quickly ran out. Most doctors' offices did not have it at all. Doctors had to delay vaccinating children while they waited for more vaccine to arrive, which made it seem as if the vaccine was scarce. The panic was fueled even more.[8]

Eventually, the Rhode Island state government decided to immunize all two hundred fifty thousand people in the state between the ages of two and twenty-two.[9] The total cost: 7 million dollars.[10]

Not Unusual

Rhode Island's experience demonstrates the impact meningitis, and the fear of it, can have on society. Although the scale and cost of the vaccinations carried out in Rhode Island were unusual, the situation was not. Wherever

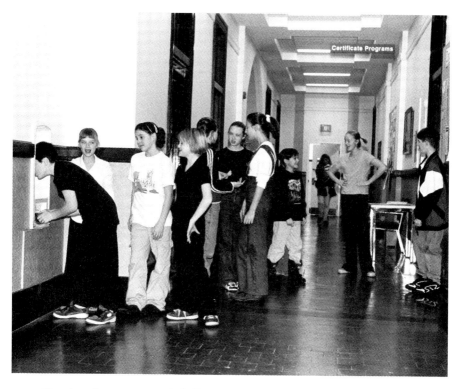

Despite what many people believe, meningitis in schools is not passed on by students drinking from public water fountains.

meningitis appears, it sparks concern—sometimes panic—and a demand for doctors to "do something."

In December 1997, for example, six cases of meningococcal disease were reported in southern Ontario, near the city of Waterloo. Two girls, Michelle Risi, sixteen, and Melissa Maharaj, eighteen, died;[11] all six cases struck people between twelve and twenty-two. As a result, the region's health officials began a crash program to vaccinate almost everyone between the ages of two and twenty-two, the age group considered at greatest risk.[12] About eighty-seven thousand people were vaccinated at enormous cost, and thousands spent a nervous few weeks wondering whether every cold was the start of a possibly fatal illness.

Schools Are Often the Sites of Scares

Fear of meningitis often has an impact on a smaller scale, too, especially when a case crops up in a school. For example, in October 1997, Noel Sheedy, seven, died of bacterial meningitis in Killaloe, Ireland. Just two months later, his cousin and playmate, Barry O'Halloran, was taken to Limerick Regional Hospital with a sports injury to his foot. He also complained of feeling generally unwell, so his doctor, Dr. Manus McGuire, recommended he undergo blood tests. Shortly after he was admitted to the hospital, his mother spotted a rash spreading over his body. Barry had meningococcemia. Fortunately, he received treatment at once and recovered. As a result of two cases of meningococcal disease coming so close together, more than one hundred people received preventative antibiotics. Killaloe Boys' National School was closed for several days.[13]

Similarly, when Jana Oliver, a student at the University of Kentucky, died of meningococcemia, health officials had to contact everyone she had encountered during the previous few days. Classmates, people who lived in her dorm, and people who attended a Super Bowl party with her were given preventative antibiotics—375 people in all. Even though hers was an isolated case, it raised concern not only at her school, but at other schools in the vicinity.[14]

Meningitis and meningococcemia also cause distress to those who are close to the victims. In March 1997, Vance Latta, twenty-five, a top athlete at Otago University in New Zealand, died of meningococcemia. His friend and athletic rival, Chris Mene, could not believe Latta was dead. "I don't think it has really hit me, because it is so hard to believe," he told a newspaper reporter. "He was such a bunch of laughs and an outgoing guy."[15]

That, unfortunately, is one of the most frightening things about meningitis and meningococcemia: They can strike anyone, even athletes as fit as Vance Latta, who had a good shot at winning the New Zealand decathlon championship. Other athletes, who had been at a party with Latta and another athlete who became ill but recovered, reacted with shock, disbelief—and fear for their own lives.

It is a response meningitis brings time after time, all over the world.

Is Fear Out of Proportion to Risk?

Although in North America meningitis and meningococcemia are not really major killers, they do claim several hundred lives each year. As the Rhode Island and Ontario experiences show, they cause fear and distress that seem to be out of proportion to the actual risk.

There are good reasons for that. "It's one of the few infectious diseases . . . that can take a healthy child or young

meningitis are very hard to tell apart in the early stages. "About half of the cases I am aware of are missed initially," he said.[19]

As a result, knowledge of the facts about the illness does not lessen parents' fear. As a mother told her local newspaper after Barry contracted bacterial meningitis in Killaloe, "At this stage, every cold and flu symptom among school-going children has become terrifying for parents. And that is understandable given the circumstances in which we find ourselves."[20]

With such strong emotions involved, meningitis can be expected to continue to cost society greatly in time, money, and concern.

Developing Countries Suffer More

In North America, meningitis outbreaks are usually limited and easily controlled. Thanks to improved vaccines, some types of meningitis have almost been eliminated. But in many countries of the world, meningitis outbreaks, caused by *Neisseria meningitidis*, often become full-scale epidemics, killing thousands. (In a typical year only 1 to 3 people out of every 100,000 in North America and Europe will develop meningococcal disease. In developing countries, 10 to 50 people per 100,000 develop the disease. During epidemics that number can rise to 500 cases per 100,000 people.[21])

Meningococcal epidemics are common in Nepal, northern India, and especially the meningitis belt of sub-Saharan Africa, which stretches across the continent from Senegal in the west to Ethiopia in the east.

Epidemics generally occur in the winter and spring in the temperate areas like Europe and Australia. In tropical countries like those in the meningitis belt, epidemics usually occur in the dry season. Young children suffer the most between epidemics, but during epidemics older children, teenagers, and young adults are also affected. Epidemics often occur about two years after a smaller outbreak. If no vaccination is carried out, epidemics can last for months.[22]

Historically, the meningitis belt has suffered epidemics every eight to twelve years. Since the 1980s, epidemics have been coming more often, but not as regularly.

In the first six months of 1996 alone, 111,280 cases of meningococcal disease and 12,840 deaths were reported in the countries that make up the African meningitis belt, the largest numbers ever reported during a single epidemic.[23] By the end of that year there had been 118,341 cases. The following year "only" 69,518 cases were reported.[24] But epidemics can be expected again unless great strides are made in preventing and controlling meningitis.

The World Health Organization, with the help of the CDC, has undertaken a large-scale project in Africa to do just that. The project includes teaching district health officers how to better identify meningitis outbreaks and conduct vaccination campaigns. Laboratories in the region are being improved. Government officials in the affected countries are being taught how to better evaluate and manage suspected epidemics.[25]

The Impact Lingers On

The impact of meningitis on society goes beyond the emotional and monetary cost of outbreaks and epidemics. There is also the cost of helping survivors deal with the aftereffects, some of which can last a lifetime.

This problem is made worse by the fact that viral meningitis can cause some of the same aftereffects as bacterial meningitis, even though it is generally considered a much less serious disease.[26] Though it is almost never fatal, it is much more common.

An estimated 30 percent of children who recover from meningitis suffer long-term aftereffects of one sort or another.[27] The National Meningitis Trust in England put together a list of the many different kinds of after effects meningitis can cause (see page 65).

We are fortunate that in North America meningitis continues to be a very rare disease. In other parts of the world, it remains a constant threat. Wherever it occurs, however, meningitis takes its toll, in money, pain, fear, and, all too often, grief.

Bacterial and Viral Meningitis Aftereffects[28]

- Balance problems
- Bouts of aggression
- Brain damage
- Clumsiness
- Deafness
- Depression
- Difficulty in concentration
- Epilepsy/seizures
- Eyesight difficulties
- General tiredness
- Giddiness
- Joint soreness/stiffness
- Learning difficulties
- Mood swings
- Recurring headaches
- Reduced ability in some areas of schoolwork
- Short-term memory lapses
- Tinnitus (ringing in the ears)
- Violent temper tantrums

7

Preventing Meningitis

Remember Virginia, whose bout with meningitis is described in Chapter 5? Although she was the one brought to the emergency room suffering from meningitis, she was not the only one who needed treatment. As soon as the diagnosis was confirmed, her doctor began assembling a list of all the people likely to have had close contact with her. It included her family, the paramedics who had brought her in, the emergency room staff, and friends who had spent the night at her house two days before. He knew that all of them would need to be treated for two days with an antibiotic. The goal would be to kill off any colonies of meningitis-causing bacteria that might be growing in their noses and throats before they could sneak into the linings of their brains and spinal cords and cause meningitis.[1]

Giving an antibiotic—specifically rifampin—to people who have had close contact with someone who has contracted meningitis caused by *Neisseria meningitidis* is the most common method used in the United States to prevent the spread of the disease.[2] In 1995, for example, nine people came down with bacterial meningitis in Mankato, Minnesota. Most of them were students at Mankato West High School or had had contact with a specific group of students at the school.

Consequently, rifampin was given to hundreds of people. The list included everyone under thirty who had lived or worked in that school district for at least seven days that year. Children who regularly attended day care there, anyone who had lived in the same house as a student from Mankato West High School that year, and steady boyfriends and girlfriends of students and faculty were also treated.[3]

Rifampin is not used to treat people who already have meningococcal disease. Instead, it helps ensure that an isolated case does not develop into a full-fledged outbreak of the disease or that an outbreak does not turn into an epidemic.

Prevention with Antibiotics

Giving preventative antibiotics to people who may be carrying meningitis-causing bacteria is called antimicrobial chemoprophylaxis. The antibiotics are usually given to persons in close contact with anyone who contracts meningococcal disease. Close contacts include people such as household members and anyone directly exposed to the patient's saliva—for example, through kissing, mouth-to-mouth resuscitation, or sharing a can of soda. In the case of small children, other children who attend the same day care center are usually given rifampin, too.[4] (In the Mankato case described earlier, rifampin was probably overused. There it was given to anyone who might have come near the patients, not just those who had close contact with them.)

It is estimated that out of every one thousand people who fall into the category of "close contact," four will develop meningococcal disease. That may not sound too worrisome, but it represents a rate of infection 500 to 800 times greater than that for the general population.[5]

Additional cases usually crop up within a few days after the first person gets sick. It is therefore important to give rifampin to close contacts as soon as possible, ideally within twenty-four hours of the first case being identified. After a couple of weeks, there is not much point to preventative treatment.[6]

Rifampin is given twice a day for two days. The dosage is determined by the age and weight of the recipient. It cannot be given to everyone, however: It is not considered safe for pregnant women, for example. It has annoying side effects, too. It turns urine, sweat, and tears reddish-orange. As a result, it can permanently discolor soft contact lenses.[7]

For people who cannot take rifampin, single doses of two other antibiotics, ciprofloxacin or ceftriaxone, are sometimes substituted. However, they have their own problems. Ciprofloxacin is not recommended for people under eighteen

People who have had close contact with a meningitis patient, by sharing eating utensils or by kissing, are given preventative antibiotic treatment.

because it has been shown to cause cartilage damage in young laboratory animals. Ceftriaxone has to be administered by injection.

Vaccines Can Help

When the meningitis outbreak occurred in Mankato, rifampin was not the only thing given to close contacts of the patients. They also received vaccinations. In fact, eventually everyone in the town received the vaccine.[8]

Unfortunately, vaccines are only available for certain types of meningitis-causing bacteria, and only certain strains of those types.

The most successful meningitis vaccine to date is one developed for the *Haemophilus influenza* type b (Hib) bacteria. Until the late 1980s, the Hib bacteria caused up to twenty-five thousand cases of meningitis in young children every year in the United States. In fact, one out of every two hundred children could be expected to develop some kind of Hib infection. (Hib most commonly causes ear and sinus infections. Besides meningitis, it can also cause skin infections, arthritis, and epiglottitis, a swelling of the throat.[9]) One out of every ten children stricken with Hib meningitis died, and many of those who survived suffered permanent disabilities.[10] Today, the disease has been virtually eliminated, thanks to the vaccine first released in the mid-1980s.

The vaccine's success is "a major medical milestone," wrote Richard Greco, a columnist for Pediatric Report's *Child Health*

Newsletter. "It is probably of the same magnitude as the polio vaccine discovery."[11]

Vaccines for Other Strains

Doctors would love to have vaccines that work as well against the *Neisseria meningitidis* and *Streptococcus pneumoniae* bacteria, the other two main causes of bacterial meningitis. Unfortunately, the existing vaccines are not as effective as the Hib vaccine.

Remember that *Neisseria meningitidis* comes in three main strains, called a, b, and c. The current vaccine is effective only against the a and c strains, plus two rarer strains, called y and w-135. (For that reason, the vaccine is formally called the a,c,y,w-135 vaccine.)

Fortunately, strain c, responsible for 45 percent of the cases in the United States, and strain a, the most common cause of epidemics in Africa,[12] are both susceptible to the vaccine. Unfortunately, strain b, which causes 46 percent of the cases in the United States and has caused at least one statewide epidemic,[13] is not. When a case of meningococcal disease caused by type b surfaces, the only way doctors have to prevent the spread of the disease is to give preventative antibiotics to close contacts of the patient.

The meningococcal vaccine currently in use in the United States is made from killed *Neisseria meningitidis* bacteria.[14] Like all other vaccines, it works by causing the body to mobilize the defenses it uses to fight off infection before a real infection takes place. The vaccine tricks the body into

A vaccine for meningitis caused by the *Haemophilus influenza* type b bacteria has successfully reduced the number of cases. However, the vaccines for meningitis caused by *Streptococcus pneumoniae* and *Neisseria meningitidis* are not as effective.

producing white blood cells and antibodies that have already been "taught" to recognize that particular bacteria. Then, if living bacteria get into the body, they are quickly destroyed before they can reproduce and cause illness.

It Does Not Always Work

Unfortunately, the meningococcal vaccine does not work on everyone, and it does not work all the time. It does not protect children younger than two years old. After two or three years the vaccine wears off, and it lasts a shorter time in children than in adults.[15]

A study conducted by the CDC during an outbreak of type c *Neisseria meningitidis* revealed that the vaccine was only about 85 percent effective in people aged two to twenty-nine. Younger children, aged two to five, were a little better off, however. The vaccine worked 93 percent of the time for them.[16]

Because the vaccine is not completely effective and because it does not last very long, vaccination usually is carried out only when there is an outbreak of meningococcal disease. If there is just an isolated case or two, vaccination is not worthwhile. And, of course, vaccination is useless if the cases are caused by strain b of *Neisseria meningitidis*.

Doctors hope that within a few years they will have vaccines that work well against all of the strains of *Neisseria meningitidis*. Once they do, the vaccine may be given to all children to prevent meningitis.

Even today, some people receive *Neisseria meningitidis* vaccinations as a matter of course. Travelers going to the meningitis belt of sub-Saharan Africa during the epidemic season are routinely vaccinated. So are soldiers, whose close, shared living quarters make them more susceptible to meningitis. People suffering from certain medical conditions such as sickle-cell anemia also routinely receive vaccinations.[17]

What Is an Outbreak of Meningitis?

Meningitis vaccinations usually are given only when there has been an outbreak of the disease. So, how do you tell an outbreak from one of the individual cases that crops up from time to time?

The answer to that question in the United States is provided by the Centers for Disease Control and Prevention, based in Atlanta. The CDC recognizes two different types of outbreak: an organization-based outbreak and a community-based outbreak.

In an organization-based outbreak, three or more confirmed or probable cases of meningococcal disease must occur within three months. All of the patients must have something in common, but must not have had any close contact with each other. Typically, they all belong to the same organization: They all go to the same school, or they are all on the same baseball team. Finally, the rate of infection has to be the equivalent of at least ten cases per one hundred thousand people.

This is calculated by dividing the number of people at risk—other people in the organization and their associates—into the number of cases, then multiplying by 100,000. For example, if there are 100 people at risk and 5 cases, you would divide 100 into 5. That equals 0.05. Then you would multiply 0.05 by 100,000, which gives you a rate of infection of 5,000 cases per 100,000—definitely an outbreak.

A community-based outbreak uses the same definition, except the people involved only live in the same area. They do not necessarily belong to the same organization. Community-based outbreaks typically occur in towns, cities, and counties.

Of course, you can have both types of outbreaks at once. Whichever type of outbreak is taking place, the CDC's recommendations are the same. First, the CDC recommends that preventative antibiotics be given to close contacts of the patients. Second, it recommends that doctors and other health

Organization-based Outbreak	Community-based Outbreak
Three or more cases occur within three months.	Three or more cases occur within three months.
All patients belong to the same organization (school, club, sports team).	All patients live in the same area.
Infection rate is at least 10 cases per 100,000 people at risk.	Infection rate is at least 10 cases per 100,000 people at risk.

care professionals be warned about the outbreak and asked to keep a sharp lookout for additional cases. Third, it recommends that the exact organism causing each case be carefully determined.

Next, the CDC recommends that the historical rate of meningitis infection in the area be examined. This helps determine whether the number of cases is unusual for that area and, if so, just how severe the outbreak is. Finally, the CDC recommends that links between cases be carefully studied to help decide who might need vaccination.[18]

The Streptococcal Vaccine

Since the early 1980s, there has also been a vaccine for the other leading bacterial cause of meningitis, *Streptococcus pneumoniae*. The *Streptococcus pneumoniae* bacterium causes between 3,000 and 6,000 cases of meningitis every year in the United States. It also causes 50,000 cases of pneumonia every year and 7 to 10 million cases of otitis media, a painful infection of the middle ear.[19] Like *Neisseria meningitidis*, *Streptococcus pneumoniae* comes in many different strains. The vaccine protects against the twenty-three most common ones.

Unfortunately, the current *Streptococcus pneumoniae* vaccine is even less effective than the *Neisseria meningitidis* one. Like the *Neisseria meningitidis* vaccine, it does not work in children under two years of age. Even in older people, it works only 60 percent of the time. Nevertheless, the CDC recommends vaccination for anyone considered at risk for *Streptococcus pneumoniae* infections, which includes elderly

The best method of preventing meningitis is good hygiene, including frequent, thorough hand washing.

people and some younger people with serious medical problems.[20]

Researchers hope to have a *Streptococcus pneumoniae* vaccine as effective as the Hib vaccine available in a few more years.

The Best Defense: Good Hygiene

For meningitis-causing bacteria for which there is no vaccine, and for all forms of viral meningitis, the only prevention is good hygiene and common sense. Wash your hands regularly, avoid sharing knives, forks, spoons, and drink containers, and cover your mouth when you sneeze or cough.

Fortunately, the organisms that cause meningitis do not live long outside the body. That means you cannot contract meningitis simply by breathing the air where a person with meningitis has been.[21]

As Nurse Mary Horne told the youngsters she vaccinated during the outbreak of type c *Neisseria meningitidis* in southern Ontario in December 1997, the best way to ensure you do not catch meningitis is to not share anything—not a cigarette, not a tube of lip gloss, not a plate of French fries. "I wouldn't want them to say we said, 'Don't kiss,'" Nurse Horne said, but she urged the teenagers to use common sense for a while.[22]

In the event of an outbreak of meningitis (or any other communicable disease), good hygiene *is* common sense.

8

Research and Future Prospects

As you have already learned, *Haemophilus influenzae* type b (Hib) vaccine has been so effective it has virtually eliminated Hib meningitis in North America, but the vaccines for *Neisseria meningitidis* and *Streptococcus pneumoniae* do not work as well.

Current meningitis research focuses primarily on developing better vaccines. There are two goals to combat *Neisseria meningitidis*: to boost the effectiveness of the current vaccine and to create a new vaccine that will also protect against type b. Thanks to genetic engineering, both goals may soon be reached.

New Vaccines Show Promise

Peter Fusco and his colleagues at North American Vaccine, a company in Beltsville, Maryland, and Denis Martin and his colleagues at Laval University Hospital Center in Quebec have separately created *Neisseria meningitidis* vaccines that show promise in animal tests and are now moving into clinical tests.[1]

Each type of *Neisseria meningitidis* bacteria has special molecules called polysaccharides, similar to sugar, which poke out from its surface. These molecules protect the bacteria from the body's immune system. Each type of meningitis bacteria has its own unique polysaccharide.[2]

The existing vaccines use mixtures of polysaccharides extracted from dead type a and c bacteria to trick the immune system into gearing up for a possible *Neisseria meningitidis* infection. But this approach does not work with type b *Neisseria meningitidis*, because its polysaccharide, polysialic acid, is too much like one that appears on some human cells. When the body discovers it in the bloodstream, it does not realize it is from an invader and should be attacked.[3]

The challenge for researchers, then, is to create a molecule different enough from the human polysaccharide to activate the immune system, while similar enough to the type b bacteria's polysaccharide to ensure the body will also attack the bacteria.

In an attempt to do that, Fusco and his colleagues changed the type b bacteria's polysaccharide slightly. Then they attached the slightly altered polysaccharide to a genetically engineered protein, also made from *Neisseria meningitidis* bacteria. They also attached polysaccharides from type a and type c bacteria. They hope they have created a vaccine that should be good against all three types.[4]

The vaccine has been tested in monkeys and seemed to work well. Booster vaccinations given months later triggered an even stronger immune response than the initial vaccination. That result tells the researchers that the monkey's immune system "memorized" the identity of the invaders, and could mean the vaccine would last longer than the current one. Scientists are currently testing the vaccine on human beings.[5]

Vaccines created by joining polysaccharides and proteins in this way are called conjugate vaccines. Conjugate vaccines for *Streptococcus pneumoniae* are also under development.

The vaccine created at Laval University Hospital is based on a slightly different approach. Instead of using polysaccharides, it uses a protein called NspA that appears on the surface of all three types of *Neisseria meningitidis* bacteria. Injections of NspA have protected mice against infections by all three types. Researchers hope it will work just as well in humans.[6]

Trying to Improve Treatment

Giving patients doses of a different protein also holds promise as a new treatment for people suffering from meningococcemia. A better form of treatment is desperately needed because even with antibiotics, meningococcemia kills 20 to 50 percent of children who contract it.[7]

Dr. Brett Giroir, assistant professor of pediatrics at the University of Texas Southwestern Medical Center in Dallas, injected children suffering from meningococcemia with extra doses of a protein found naturally in white blood cells.

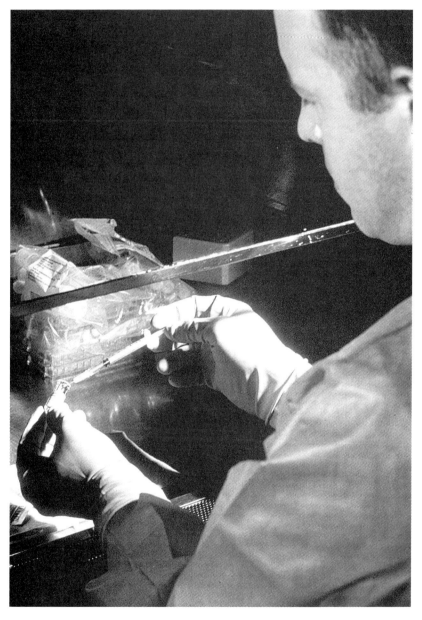

Researchers are working on the development of new meningitis vaccines.

This protein is used by the white blood cells to kill the *Neisseria meningitidis* bacteria and neutralize their toxins. Unfortunately, the body is not able to produce enough of it naturally to fight off meningococcal disease by itself. The researchers hoped that providing extra doses of the protein would pick up the slack.[8]

Results of the preliminary study were very encouraging and research continues. Twenty-six patients between the ages of one and eighteen were given the drug at six Texas medical centers. Only one died. Normally, doctors would have expected eight or nine of the children to die.[9]

Fighting Viral Meningitis

Researchers are also looking for better ways to fight viral meningitis. Unlike bacterial meningitis, viral meningitis cannot be treated with antibiotics, and there are no vaccines for it. Fortunately, viral meningitis is not as serious as bacterial meningitis, but it still makes people very sick and can cause long-term aftereffects. It is particularly dangerous for infants less than a year old. It is also much more common.

Recently, researchers have been testing a new virus-killing drug called pleconaril against viral meningitis. In trials in the United States, Australia, and South Africa in 1996, the drug cut the length of time people suffered from the disease by more than half.[10] Additional trials are continuing. Doctors may soon have something more effective to give patients with viral meningitis than just pain-relievers.

Fighting Meningitis Around the World

Better vaccines and better ways to treat meningitis will certainly help the developing countries that suffer most from the disease. However, even greater strides can be made by improving the ways in which those countries deal with epidemics.

In 1996 a team of health officials from the World Health Organization and the CDC's Division of Bacterial and Mycotic Diseases (DBMD) visited several countries in Africa's meningitis belt to see how capable they were of dealing with an epidemic. Based on the information they gathered, the experts developed a training program for local health officials to help them better identify and monitor epidemics.[11]

In addition, efforts are under way to improve laboratories in the region and to find ways to better prevent and control meningitis. The countries involved often do not have the resources for mass vaccination, the best way to control or even prevent an epidemic.[12]

The hope is that all these efforts will reduce the illness and death caused by meningitis in the region. It may also help the countries deal better with epidemics of diseases such as yellow fever, measles, and cholera.[13]

It Is Not Going Away

Despite all these efforts, meningitis will not vanish soon. The bacteria and viruses that cause it are all around us, in our throats and noses and stomachs and intestines. Too little is known about why some people get meningitis and others do not. There is still a lot of research to be done.

Nevertheless, great strides have already been made in North America in reducing the toll of meningitis in all its forms. By almost wiping out the form of meningitis most common in children, the Hib vaccine has raised the average age of bacterial meningitis patients from fifteen months to twenty-five years. That means bacterial meningitis is now more of a disease of adults than of children.[14]

Unfortunately, clusters of meningococcal disease caused by the type c *Neisseria meningitidis* bacteria are becoming more common. No one knows why. It may just be part of a natural cycle in the bacteria's evolution.[15] Although vaccines can prevent epidemics, they do not help the primary cases, the first people to come down with meningitis during an outbreak. Every year, the disease kills young, otherwise healthy people who might have enjoyed a long life.

In December 1997, bacterial meningitis killed two teenaged girls and sickened four other people in Ontario. In January 1998, two New Jersey children and a casino dealer died in unrelated cases. In the winter of 1996–97, the disease killed three college students and a high school athlete in Michigan and a student at Fordham University in New York, two elementary-school girls in Orange County, California, and two toddlers and a four-year-old boy who were cared for by the same baby-sitter in New Jersey. A year earlier, outbreaks in Arkansas, Oklahoma, Missouri, and Florida killed eight people. In Oregon and parts of Washington State, cases have more than tripled during the past two years.

The list goes on and on. In all, cases of meningococcal disease increased 47 percent from 1986 to 1996.[16]

The United States' battle against meningitis may be "a remarkable public-health success," as the CDC's Dr. Bradley Perkins said,[17] but that does not mean doctors or the public can afford to forget about it.

"It is a very, very bad disease and we don't have a good approach to it," said Dr. Gregory Storch, a pediatric infectious-disease specialist at Washington University School of Medicine in St. Louis. "So it's certainly a matter of concern that it is increasing."[18]

The battle goes on.

Q & A

Q. What are meningitis and meningococcemia?

A. Meningitis is an inflammation of the meninges, the linings of the brain and spinal cord. Many things, including bacteria, viruses, fungi, and even head injuries, can cause it. One of the most dangerous causes is a bacterium called *Neisseria meningitidis*. Sometimes this bacterium infects not only the meninges, but also the bloodstream. Any infection of the body by *Neisseria meningitidis* is called meningococcal disease. When it infects the bloodstream, either as a complication of meningitis or directly, the result is a very deadly disease called meningococcemia. It can kill within hours by poisoning organs throughout the body and causing internal bleeding.

Q. Why is it so important to look for a rash in a case of suspected meningitis, and what does the rash look like?

A. The rash is a key indicator that septicemia (a blood infection) has developed, and it means the person has to be rushed to the nearest emergency room. Typically, the rash associated with a meningococcal infection starts as a flat rash (no bumps) of tiny red spots that do not turn white when you press on the skin. As the infection gets worse, it becomes purplish splotches. However, rashes can look different on different people. Any rash associated with a headache and fever should be checked by a doctor at once.

Q. Can I catch meningitis just by being in the same room with someone who has it?

A. No. Although meningitis is contagious, none of the organisms that cause it can live very long outside the body. The people at risk for catching meningitis are those who have had close contact with someone who has it, especially if they have kissed, shared cigarettes or eating utensils, or drunk out of the same glass or other container.

Q. Where do the bacteria and viruses that cause meningitis come from?

A. Most of them come from inside your own body. The bacteria that cause bacterial meningitis live in the back of the nose and throat in between 10 and 25 percent of the population. You could be carrying these bacteria right now and not know it. They only cause meningitis in a very small percentage of people—no one knows why. The viruses that most commonly cause meningitis live in the digestive system.

Q. Can anyone get meningitis?

A. Yes, although children under age five, people aged sixteen to twenty-five, and people fifty-five and older are the most susceptible.

Q. I have heard of "cold season" and "flu season." Is there such a thing as "meningitis season?"

A. Bacterial and viral meningitis can occur at any time, but bacterial meningitis is more common in the winter months (November to March). Viral meningitis is most common in the summer.

Q. A spinal tap sounds awful. Does it hurt?

A. It is not as painful as it sounds. In some cases, it is only mildly uncomfortable. The skin in the lower back is not particularly sensitive and the needle used is extremely slender. Besides, the skin is often numbed before the needle is inserted. Sometimes people who have had a spinal tap get a headache after the procedure is over, but it can usually be alleviated by lying down.

Q. When there were a couple of cases of meningitis in my hometown, doctors kept saying that although there had been an increase in the number of cases, there was no outbreak. What is the difference?

A. Cases of meningitis do not qualify as an outbreak unless there are a higher-than-normal number of them within a specific group or community, and the cases are all related. An outbreak, in other words, means that people are transmitting the disease to each other. Sometimes several cases that are not related to each other crop up at once, just through bad luck. Usually vaccinations are only administered if there has been an outbreak, not if there have just been a few extra unrelated cases.

Q. What is the best way to keep from getting meningitis?

A. Stay as healthy as possible by eating well and getting plenty of rest and exercise. Wash your hands frequently, especially before eating and after using the bathroom. Do not share cups, knives, forks, spoons, glasses, or your toothbrush with anyone else. Do not rub your eyes and nose; that can help germs penetrate the mucus linings. In other words, the best way to keep from getting meningitis is to practice the same good health habits that keep you from getting colds, influenza, and other communicable diseases.

Q. Why are people so scared of meningitis?

A. Meningitis is scary because, although it is rare, it can strike anyone at any time and can kill a healthy child or young adult in just a few hours. It is also scary because its initial symptoms are much the same as influenza, which means people sometimes wait too long to get help.

Meningitis Timeline

Pre-1800—Meningitis is lumped together with many other diseases under the name "brain fever." Meningitis epidemics occurred every ten to twelve years.

1806—Dr. Vieussuex identifies bacterial meningitis as a separate disease. At the time, bacterial meningitis was almost always fatal.

1887—Anton Weichselbaum identifies *Neisseria meningitidis* as the cause of meningococcal meningitis, the form of the disease that causes epidemics.

1906—Dr. G. Jochmann makes the first antiserum for meningococcal meningitis. It is the first effective treatment. The death rate for some strains of bacterial meningitis drops from 80 percent to 30 percent.

1914 –1918—Meningitis epidemics occur in all the countries involved in World War I, hitting military forces the hardest.

1928—A major epidemic breaks out in China and spreads around the world. Existing antiserum is useless against it.

1932—Gerhard Domagk discovers sulfanilamide, the first antibiotic that is effective against bacterial meningitis.

1970s—A vaccine for *Neisseria meningitidis* is introduced. It only works against two of the three most common strains.

1980s—A vaccine for *Streptococcus pneumoniae*, another leading cause of meningitis, is introduced.

1985—A vaccine for *Haemophilus influenzae* type b (Hib), the leading cause of meningitis in infants, is introduced. It only works in children two and older.

1987—An improved Hib vaccine that works in all children is introduced and widely adopted.

1986 –1995—The number of cases of Hib meningitis drops 94 percent.

1996—The worst meningitis epidemic in history occurs in the meningitis belt of sub-Saharan Africa. There are 111,280 cases and 12,840 deaths.

For More Information

Centers for Disease Control and Prevention
National Center for Infectious Diseases
1600 Clifton Road, N.E.
Atlanta, GA 30333
404-639-3311
<http://www.cdc.gov>

Meningitis Foundation of America, Inc.
7155 Shadeland Station, Suite 190
Indianapolis, IN 46256-3922
800-668-1129
<http://www.musa.org>

Meningitis Research Foundation
13 High Street
Thornbury, Bristol, UK
BS35 2AE
<http://www.meningitis.org>

Chapter Notes

Chapter 1. A Fast, Deadly Disease

1. Diana Brahams, "Meningitis, Schools, and Public Alarm," *The Lancet*, June 20, 1992, p. 1532.

2. University of Toronto, "Meningitis," *Health News*, June 1989, p. 1.

3. Tony Dajer, "Firestorm," *Discover*, vol. 17, no. 6, June 1996, p. 38.

4. Centers for Disease Control and Prevention, "Outbreak of Aseptic Meningitis—Whiteside County, Illinois, 1995," *Mortality and Morbidity Weekly Report*, vol. 46, no. 10, March 14, 1997, p. 221.

5. University of Toronto, p. 1.

6. Government of Hawaii, *Department of Health Web Site*, n.d., <http://www.hawaii.gov/health/eddmenin.htm> (May 1, 1998).

7. Centers for Disease Control and Prevention, "Control and Prevention of Meningococcal Disease: Recommendations of the Advisory Committee on Immunization Practices," *Morbidity and Mortality Weekly Report*, February 14, 1997, p. 1.

8. Charles A. Pohl, "Practical Approach to Bacterial Meningitis in Childhood," *American Family Physician*, vol. 47, no. 7, May 15, 1993, p. 1604.

9. CDC/NCID, "DBMD Works to Control Meningitis in Africa," *Focus*, March–April 1997, <http://www.cdc.gov/ncidod/focus/vol6no2/dbmd.htm> (January 27, 1999).

Chapter 2. Meningitis Through the Ages

1. "Oscar Wilde," *Microsoft Encarta*, 1994, <http://encarta.msn.com/EncartaHome.asp> (December 7, 1998).

2. "Helen Keller," *TimesDaily*, n.d., <http://timesdaily.com/keller.html> (May 1, 1998).

3. Charles A. Pohl, "Practical Approach to Bacterial Meningitis in Childhood," *American Family Physician*, vol. 47, no. 7, May 15, 1993, p. 1595.

4. Sara F. Branham, "A Defense of Epimetheus: Development of Knowledge Concerning the Meningococcus," *Journal of the American Medical Women's Association*, vol. 15, no. 6, June 1960, p. 571.

5. Louis J. Vorhaus, "Meningitis," *Microsoft Encarta*, 1994, <http://encarta.msn.com/EncartaHome.asp> (December 7, 1998).

6. Branham, p. 572.

7. Ibid.

8. Ibid.

9. Ibid.

10. Wayne Biddle, *A Field Guide to Germs* (New York: Henry Holt and Company, 1995), p. 101.

11. Branham, p. 573.

12. "Domagk, Gerhard Johannes Paul," *Microsoft Encarta Concise Encyclopedia*, On-Line Edition, <http://encarta.msn.com> (December 7, 1998).

13. Ibid.

14. Branham, p. 574.

15. Pohl.

16. Biddle, p. 100.

17. Ibid., p. 101.

18. Andy Coghlan, "Monkeys Boost Meningitis Hopes," *New Scientist*, May 24, 1997, <http://www.newscientist.com/ns/970524/menin.html> (May 1, 1998).

19. John Bowersox, "Group B. Strep Vaccine Shows Promise in Clinical Studies," *National Institute of Allergy and Infectious Diseases Press Release*, November 20, 1996, <http://www.niaid.gov/newsroom/gbsvacc.htm> (December 7, 1998).

20. Coghlan.

21. "The *Hemophilus influenzae* type b (Hib) Vaccine—Long-term Research Pays Off," *Meningitis Foundation of America Web Site*, n.d., <http://www.musa.org/hib1.htm> (May 1, 1998).

22. "Health Report," *Time*, vol. 150, no. 15, October 13, 1997, p. 24.

23. *Meningitis Foundation of America Web Site*.

24. Ibid.

25. Ibid.

26. Linda A. Johnson, "Very, Very Bad: Deadly Bacterial Meningitis Sneaks in, Looking Like the Flu," *Associated Press*, April 14, 1998.

27. Ibid.

Chapter 3. What Is Meningitis?

1. Dr. John Lockley, *Headaches: The Complete Guide to Relieving Headaches and Migraine* (London: Bloomsbury Publishing Ltd., 1994), pp. 94–95.

2. Tony Dajer, "Vital Signs: Firestorm," *Discover*, vol. 17, no. 6, June 1996, p. 38.

3. Ibid.

4. Amy Holm, Chris Hammerbeck, and Betsy Giese, "Bacterial Meningitis," n.d., <http://www.uwrf.edu/~cg04/physiology/mening5.html> (May 1, 1998).

5. Ibid.

6. Centers for Disease Control and Prevention, "Summary of Notifiable Diseases, United States, 1994," *Mortality and Morbidity Weekly Report*, vol. 43, no. 53, 1995, p. 71.

7. Centers for Disease Control and Prevention, "Outbreak of Aseptic Meningitis—Whiteside County, Illinois, 1995," *Mortality and Morbidity Weekly Report*, vol. 46, no. 10, March 14, 1997, p. 221.

8. Holm et al.

9. Lockley, pp. 92–93.

10. Linda A. Johnson, "Very, Very Bad: Deadly Bacterial Meningitis Sneaks in, Looking Like the Flu," *Associated Press*, April 14, 1998.

11. Ibid.

12. Ibid.

13. John Saunders, "Young Ontarians Line up for Shots: Meningitis Scare Prompts Immunization Campaign after Six Cases of the Disease Surfaced," *Toronto Globe and Mail*, December 30, 1997, p. A4.

14. Holm et al.

15. Johnson.

16. Lockley, p. 93.

17. Abigail Zuger, "Meningitis Mystery," *Discover*, vol. 15, no. 3, March 1994, p. 40.

18. Ibid.

19. Ibid.

Chapter 4. Diagnosis of Meningitis

1. Dr. John Lockley, *Headaches: The Complete Guide to Relieving Headaches and Migraine* (London: Bloomsbury Publishing Ltd., 1994), p. 94.

2. Ibid.

3. Barbara Apgar, "Clinical Features of Acute Bacterial Meningitis in Adults," *American Family Physician*, vol. 56, no. 4, September 15, 1997, p. 1191.

4. Lockley, p. 94.

5. Charles A. Pohl, "Practical Approach to Bacterial Meningitis in Childhood," *American Family Physician*, vol. 47, no. 7, May 15, 1993, p. 1595.

6. "Meningitis Symptoms," *Meningitis Foundation of America Web Site*, n.d., <http://www.musa.org/symptoms.htm> (May 1, 1998).

7. Tony Dajer, "Vital Signs: Firestorm," *Discover*, vol. 17, no. 6, June 1996, p. 38.

8. The Nemours Foundation, "Fluid Sample Tests: Lumbar Puncture (also called Spinal Tap)," *Kidshealth.org Web Site*, n.d., <http://kidshealth.org/parent/healthy/labtests/labtest9.html> (May 1, 1998).

9. Dajer, p. 38.

10. The Nemours Foundation.

11. University of Toronto, "Meningitis," *Health News*, vol. 7, no. 3, June 1989, p. 1.

12. The Nemours Foundation.

13. Robert Berkow, editor-in-chief, *The Merck Manual of Medical Information, Home Edition* (Whitehouse Station, N.J.: Merck Research Laboratories, 1997), p. 374.

14. The Nemours Foundation.

15. Ibid.

16. Ibid.

17. Karen Lee Ziner, "'Then They . . . Told Me He Was Going to Die,'" *Providence Journal-Bulletin*, February 28, 1998, p. A1.

18. Amy Holm, Chris Hammerbeck, and Betsy Giese, "Bacterial Meningitis," n.d., <http://www.uwrf.edu/~cg04/physiology/mening5.html> (May 1, 1998).

19. "Top 20 Meningitis FAQs," *Meningitis Foundation of America Web Site*, n.d., <http://www.musa.org/faqs.htm> (May 1, 1998).

20. Ziner, p. A1.

Chapter 5. Treatment of Meningitis

1. Tony Dajer, "Vital Signs: Firestorm," *Discover*, vol. 17, no. 6, June 1996, p. 38.

2. Ibid.

3. University of Toronto, "Meningitis," *Health News*, vol. 7, no. 3, June 1989, p. 3.

4. Dr. John Lockley, *Headaches: The Complete Guide to Relieving Headaches and Migraine* (London: Bloomsbury Publishing Ltd., 1994), p. 96.

5. Ibid., p. 95.

6. Charles A. Pohl, "Practical Approach to Bacterial Meningitis in Childhood," *American Family Physician,* vol. 47, no. 7, May 15, 1993, p. 1595.

7. Dajer, p. 38.

8. Lockley, p. 95.

9. Division of Bacterial and Mycotic Diseases, "Bacterial Meningitis," *Centers for Disease Control and Prevention Web Site,* n.d., <http://www.cdc.gov/ncidod/dbmd/bactmen.htm> (May 1, 1998).

10. Robert Berkow, editor-in-chief, *The Merck Manual of Medical Information, Home Edition* (Whitehouse Station, N.J.: Merck Research Laboratories, 1997), p. 374.

11. Pohl, p. 1595.

12. Dr. P. P. Ashok, "Meningitis," n.d., <http://www.exicom.org/bio_med/julaug96/menin.htm> (May 1, 1998).

13. Dajer, p. 38.

Chapter 6. Meningitis and Society

1. Felice J. Freyer, "Deaths, Fear Fueled Panic," *The Providence Journal-Bulletin,* March 1, 1998, p. 1A.

2. Ibid.

3. Elizabeth Rau, "Almond, Health Officials: Don't Panic," *The Providence Journal-Bulletin,* February 28, 1998, p. 6A.

4. Freyer, p. 1A.

5. Ibid.

6. Ibid.

7. Ibid.

8. Ibid.

9. Jonathan D. Rockoff, "Meningitis Fear Lessens; Clinics to Open This Week," *The Providence Journal-Bulletin,* March 1, 1998, p. 1A.

10. Freyer, p. 1A.

11. "Meningitis Scare," *Maclean's*, vol. 111, no. 2, January 12, 1998, p. 19.

12. Ibid.

13. Martina Scanlan, "Meningitis Scare Sweeps East Clare," *The Clare Champion Online*, December 5, 1997, <http://www.clarechampion.ie/97/dec/mening.htm> (January 27, 1999).

14. Jake Burgess, "Student Death at UK Raises Concerns at MSU," *The Murray State News*, n.d., <http://www.thenews.org/0216/ndeath.htm> (May 1, 1998).

15. "Top Athlete Dies: Meningitis Hits After Champs," *New Zealand News UK*, March 26, 1997, <http://www.nzewsuk.co.uk/26mar97/lead.html> (May 1, 1998).

16. Linda A. Johnson, "Very, Very Bad: Deadly Bacterial Meningitis Sneaks in, Looking Like the Flu," *Associated Press*, April 14, 1998.

17. Freyer, p. A1.

18. Ibid.

19. "Girl, 12, Dies of Meningitis," *The Chattanooga Times*, February 7, 1998, <http://www.chattimes.com/news/today/Saturday/February71998/CTStorym2sick02.html> (March 2, 1999).

20. Scanlan.

21. "Case Report *Neisseria Meningitidis* Serogroup A in Ontario," *Canada Communicable Disease Report*, vol. 23, no. 18, September 15, 1997, <http://hwcweb.hwc.ca/hpb/lcdc/publicat/ccdr/97vol23/dr2318eb.html> (January 27, 1999).

22. Ibid.

23. CDC/NCID, "DBMD Works to Control Meningitis in Africa," *Focus*, March–April 1997, <http://www.cdc.gov/ncidod/focus/vol6no2/dbmd.htm> (January 27, 1999).

24. WHO/OMS "Disease Outbreaks Reported: Meningitis in Chad," *Emerging and Other Communicable Diseases Surveillance and Control*, n.d. <http://www.who.ch/emc/outbreak_news/n1998/apr/n22apr1998.html> (May 1, 998).

25. CDC/NCID.

26. "Recovery," *Meningitis Foundation of America Web Site*, n.d., <http://www.musa.org/recovery.htm> (May 1, 1998).

27. Charles A. Pohl, "Practical Approach to Bacterial Meningitis in Childhood," *American Family Physician*, vol. 47, no. 7, May 15, 1993, p. 1595.

28. Ibid.

Chapter 7. Preventing Meningitis

1. Tony Dajer, "Firestorm," *Discover*, vol. 17, no. 6, June 1996, p. 38.

2. CDC, "Control and Prevention of Meningococcal Disease" and "Control and Prevention of Serogroup C Meningococcal Disease: Evaluation and Management of Suspected Outbreaks: Recommendations of the Advisory Committee on Immunization Practices (ACIP)," *Morbidity and Mortality Weekly Report Recommendations and Reports*, vol. 46, no. RR-5, February 14, 1997, <http://www.cdc.gov/epo/mmwr/preview/ind97_rr.html> (January 27, 1999).

3. "Meningitis Outbreak in Mankato, Minnesota, January–February 1995," n.d., <http://www.uwrf.edu/~cg04/physiology/mankato.html> (May 1, 1998).

4. CDC.

5. Ibid.

6. Ibid.

7. Ibid.

8. "Meningitis Outbreak in Mankato."

9. Richard Greco, "Media Ignore Historic Medical Event," *Pediatric Report's Child Health Newsletter*, vol. 7, no. 11, January 1991, p. 86.

10. National Institute of Allergy and Infectious Diseases, "The *Hemophilus Influenzae* Type b (Hib) Vaccine—Long-term Research Pays Off," *Meningitis Foundation of America Web Site*, July 17, 1996, <http://www.musa.org/hib1.htm> (May 1, 1998).

11. Greco, p. 86.

12. CDC.

13. Ibid.

14. "Questions and Answers about Meningitis," *The Providence Journal-Bulletin*, March 5, 1998, p. B5.

15. CDC.

16. The American Association for the Advancement of Science, "Vaccine Takes on Meningitis—But Well Enough?," *ScienceNOW*, February 10, 1998, <http://sciencenow.sciencemag.org/archives. 298.shtml> (January 27, 1999).

17. Wayne Biddle, *A Field Guide to Germs*, (New York: Henry Holt and Company, 1995), p. 102.

18. CDC.

19. Martin Cetron, Jay Butler, Dan Jernigan, Martha Alexander, Sandra Roush, and Robert Breiman, "CDC Chapter on Pneumococcal Disease," *Meningitis Foundation of America Web Site*, n.d., <http://www.musa.org/pneumoco.htm> (May 1, 1998).

20. Ibid.

21. The Division of Bacterial and Mycotic Diseases, National Center for Infectious Diseases, Centers for Disease Control and Prevention, "Bacterial Meningitis," *CDC Web Site*, n.d., <http://www.cdc.gov/ncidod/dbmd/bactmen.htm> (May 1, 1998).

22. John Saunders, "Young Ontarians Line up for Shots: Meningitis Scare Prompts Immunization Campaign After Six Cases of the Disease Surfaced," *Toronto Globe and Mail*, December 30, 1997, p. A4.

Chapter 8. Research and Future Prospects

1. Andy Coghlan, "Monkeys Boost Meningitis Hopes," *New Scientist*, May 24, 1997, <http://www.newscientist.com/ns/ 970524/menin.html> (May 1, 1998).

2. Ibid.

3. Ibid.

4. Ibid.

5. Ibid.

6. Ibid.

7. Ellen Mayou, "Study Led by UT Southwestern Finds Promising New Treatment for Meningococcemia," *University of Texas Southwestern Medical Center Press Release*, November 13, 1997, <http://www.swmed.edu/home_page/news/giroir.htm> (December 8, 1998).

8. Ibid.

9. Ibid.

10. Ibid.

11. CDC/NCID, "DBMD Works to Control Meningitis in Africa," *Focus*, March–April 1997, <http://www.cdc.gov/ncidod/focus/vol6no2/dbmd.htm> (January 27, 1999).

12. Ibid.

13. Ibid.

14. Anne Schuchat, Katherine Robinson, Jay D. Wenger, Lee H. Harrison, Monica Farley, Arthur L. Reingold, Lewis Lefkowitz, and Bradley A. Perkins, "Bacterial Meningitis in the United States in 1995," *The New England Journal of Medicine*, vol. 337, no. 14, October 2, 1997, p. 970.

15. Linda A. Johnson, "Very, Very Bad: Deadly Bacterial Meningitis Sneaks in, Looking Like the Flu," *Associated Press*, April 14, 1998.

16. Ibid.

17. Ibid.

18. Ibid.

Glossary

antibiotic—A substance that can destroy or inhibit the growth of bacteria. Antibiotics used against meningitis include ceftriaxone, cefotaxime, ampicillin, and vancomycin.

antibody—A protein substance produced in the blood or tissues that destroys or weakens a specific bacterium, virus, or poison.

antimicrobial chemoprophylaxis—Giving antibiotics to people exposed to particular bacteria to destroy colonies of the bacteria before they can cause disease or be passed on to other people. For meningitis, an antibiotic called rifampin is given.

antiserum—*See* serum therapy.

aseptic meningitis—Meningitis caused by a virus instead of a bacterium.

bacteria—Self-contained microscopic organisms that eat, excrete, and reproduce.

blood-brain barrier—A mechanism that prevents certain potentially harmful substances from entering brain tissue while allowing others to enter freely.

booster—A supplementary dose of a vaccine.

cerebrospinal fluid (CSF)—A fluid that bathes the surface of the brain and spinal cord, nourishing them and acting as a shock absorber.

communicable—*See* contagious.

contagious—Able to be transmitted from one person to another.

corticosteroid—A drug given to meningitis patients to reduce the inflammation of the meninges.

cribriform plate—A bony plate through which the nerves that transmit our sense of smell pass into the brain.

Cryptoccocus neoformans—A fungus that grows in the soil worldwide and can cause meningitis in people with depressed immune systems.

CT scanner—Computerized axial tomography scanner, a device that produces cross-sectional views of the inside of a body.

cultures—Living material that is grown in a prepared nutrient mixture.

cytokines—Chemicals white blood cells release to communicate with each other and control the body's immune response.

epidemic—An outbreak of a contagious disease that spreads rapidly and widely.

Escherichia coli—A common bacterium that sometimes causes meningitis in newborn babies.

fungus—An organism, usually considered a plant, that does not have chlorophyll. Fungi include molds, mildews, and yeasts.

genetic engineering—Altering the structure of the genetic material in a living organism to achieve a desired result. For example, altering a bacterium so that it produces a special protein needed to make a new kind of meningitis vaccine.

Group B streptococcus—A common bacterium that can cause meningitis in newborn children.

Haemophilus influenzae **type b**—Until recently, the most common cause of bacterial meningitis in children. A vaccine introduced in the mid-1980s has almost eliminated it in North America.

immune system—The body's many different methods of identifying and destroying invading organisms and substances.

lumbar puncture—*See* spinal tap.

meninges—The linings of the brain and spinal cord. The meninges consist of three parts: the dura mater, a tough outer layer; the pia mater, a fine, meshlike inner layer; and the loose-fitting arachnoid layer, which contains the cerebrospinal fluid.

meningitis belt—A broad area of Africa, stretching east to west across the continent just south of the Sahara Desert, where meningitis epidemics occur regularly.

meningococcemia—A serious, sometimes deadly infection of the blood caused by *Neisseria meningitidis*. It sometimes develops at the same time as meningococcal meningitis.

Neisseria meningitidis—One of the species of bacteria that most commonly causes meningitis, and the only one that causes epidemics of the disease.

outbreak—The occurrence of several related cases of meningitis within a short period.

polysaccharides—Sugary molecules on the surface of bacteria that protect the bacteria from the immune system but also help trigger the immune response.

protozoa—One-celled organisms that sometimes cause disease.

seizure—An intense, involuntary muscle contraction.

septicemia—A dangerous buildup of toxins in the blood caused by a systemwide infection.

serum—The liquid part of blood. It is a clear, yellowish liquid.

serum therapy—Injecting serum from a human or animal that has developed antibodies to a particular virus or bacterium into another human or animal to make them immune to that particular germ. This antibody-containing serum is called antiserum.

spinal tap—Also known as a lumbar puncture. The process of inserting a needle into the lower region of the spine and drawing samples of the cerebrospinal fluid, to see if it is infected with meningitis-causing organisms.

Staphylococcus aureus—A common bacterium that sometimes causes meningitis, usually as a complication of a surgical procedure.

Streptococcus pneumoniae—One of the three types of bacteria that most commonly causes meningitis.

syphilis—A disease, usually transmitted sexually, which if left untreated can lead to a variety of neurological problems, including meningitis.

tuberculosis—An infectious disease caused by a bacterium. It usually affects the lungs, but meningitis is a possible complication.

vaccine—A preparation of a disease-causing organism or its products that causes the immune system to gear up to fight that organism. This protects the person who receives the vaccine from infection by the actual organism in the future.

virus—An organism that is unable to reproduce on its own. Instead, it invades living cells and tricks them into producing hundreds of new viruses, which spill out when the cell bursts and dies.

Further Reading

Books

Berkow, Robert, editor-in-chief. *The Merck Manual of Medical Information, Home Edition.* Whitehouse Station, N.J.: Merck Research Laboratories, 1997, pp. 372–376.

Biddle, Wayne. *A Field Guide to Germs.* New York: Henry Holt and Company, 1995, p. 101.

Cartwright, Keith, ed. *Meningococcal Disease.* New York: John Wiley, 1995.

Articles

Adams, Richard M. "Meningitis and Encephalitis: Diseases that Attack the Brain." *Current Health*, vol. 21, no. 2, October 1994, p. 27.

The American Association for the Advancement of Science. "Vaccine Takes on Meningitis—But Well Enough?" *Science NOW*, February 10, 1998.

Brahams, Diana. "Meningitis, Schools, and Public Alarm." *The Lancet*, June 20, 1992, p. 1532.

Dajer, Tony. "Firestorm." *Discover*, vol. 17, no. 6, June 1996, p. 38.

Greco, Richard. "Media Ignore Historic Medical Event." *Pediatric Report's Child Health Newsletter*, vol. 7, no. 11, January 1991, p. 86.

"Questions and Answers about Meningitis." *The Providence Journal-Bulletin*, March 5, 1998.

Ziner, Karen Lee. "'Then They . . . Told Me He Was Going to Die.'" *Providence Journal-Bulletin*, February 28, 1998.

Zuger, Abigail. "Meningitis Mystery." *Discover*, vol. 15, no. 3, March 1994, p. 40.

Internet Addresses

Healthcare Computing Publications, Inc. and Margorie Lazoff. "Acute Bacterial Meningitis." *Medical Computing Today Archives.* 1997–1998. <http://www.medicalcomputingtoday.com/0nvabm.html> (February 25, 1999).

The Nemours Foundation. "Meningitis." *KidsHealth.org Childhood Infections.* January 20, 1998. <http://kidshealth.org/parent/common/meningitis.html> (February 25, 1999).

The Meningitis Foundation of America, Inc. *Meningitis Foundation of America.* 1998. <http://www.musa.org> (February 25, 1999).

National Meningitis Trust Web Site. n.d. <http://www.meningitis-trust.org.uk> (February 25, 1999).

WHO/OMS. "Cerebrospinal Meningitis." *Emerging and Other Communicable Diseases Surveillance and Control.* 1998. <http://www.who.int/emc/diseases/meningitis/index.html> (February 25, 1999).

Index

Hib. *See Haemophilus influenzae* type b.
HIV/AIDS, 36
Horne, Mary, 78
hydrocephalus, 53

I

ibuprofen allergy, 38
impaired consciousness, 40
influenza, 32

J

Jochmann, Dr. G., 16

K

Keller, Helen, 12, 14
Kile, Dale, 60
Killaloe, Ireland, 58

L

lumbar puncture. *See* spinal tap.
Lyme disease, 37–38

M

Mankato, Minnesota, 67, 68, 70
Martin, Denis, 79, 81
Meier, Frederick, 41
meninges, 8, 25
meningitis
    aftereffects, 9, 21, 47, 53, 64–65, 70
    causes of, 8, 15, 25–29, 31–32, 34–38
    diagnosis, 39–47
    effects on society, 54–60, 62–64
    fear of, 54–60, 62–64
meningitis belt, 9, 62–63, 74
meningococcal disease, 9, 54–55, 58, 67, 73–74, 83
meningococccmia, 31, 41, 48, 54, 58–59, 81

N

Naegleria fowleri, 37
National Meningitis Trust, 64
Neisseria meningitidis, 8–9, 15–21, 27, 41, 46, 62, 67, 71, 73–74, 76, 78, 79–81, 83, 85
neonatal meningitis, 34–35
NspA, 81

O

outbreak, 74–76
    community-based outbreak, 74–76
    organization-based outbreak, 74–76

P

penicillin, 19, 51–52
Perkins, Bradley, 23, 60, 86
pia mater, 25
pleconaril, 83
pneumococcal meningitis, 46
polysaccharides, 22, 80–81
polysialic acid, 80
prevention, 31–32, 66–68, 70–71, 73–76, 78
Prontosil, 18
protozoa, 8, 25, 37

R

rash, 7, 41, 46–47, 58
rate of infection, calculating, 74–75
Rhode Island, 54–56
rifampin, 67–68, 70

S

Schuchat, Ann, 32
septic shock, 31
scrum therapy, 15–18
spinal meningitis, 25

111